LT & me

LT&me

What raising a champion taught me about

life, faith, and listening to your dreams

Loreane Tomlinson
with Patti M. Britton & Ginger Kolbaba

Tyndale House Publishers, Inc., Carol Stream, Illinois

Visit Tyndale's exciting Web site at www.tyndale.com

TYNDALE and Tyndale's quill logo are registered trademarks of Tyndale House Publishers, Inc.

LT & Me: What Raising a Champion Taught Me about Life, Faith, and Listening to Your Dreams

Copyright © 2009 by Loreane Tomlinson. All rights reserved.

Cover photo of LaDainian and Loreane Tomlinson copyright © by Walsh Photography. All rights reserved.

Interior photo of LaDainian playing for TCU courtesy of Texas Christian University. Reprinted with permission.

Interior photo of LaDainian in his San Diego Chargers uniform copyright © by Mike Nowak/ San Diego Chargers. All rights reserved.

Interior photo of LaDainian scoring his 100th touchdown copyright © by AP Images. All rights reserved.

Interior photo of LaDainian scoring his first touchdown against the Chiefs copyright © by Donald Miralle/Getty Images. All rights reserved.

Interior photo of LaDainian scoring his 111th rushing touchdown copyright © by AP Images. All rights reserved.

Interior photo of LaDainian doing charity work copyright © Howard Lipin/San Diego Union Tribune. All rights reserved.

Interior photo of LaDainian receiving an award at the 2007 ESPYs copyright © by AP Images. All rights reserved.

All other interior photos are from the Tomlinson family collection and are used by permission.

Designed by Dean H. Renninger

Published in association with the literary agency of Queen Literary Agency, Inc., 850 Seventh Avenue, Suite 704, New York, New York 10019.

All Scripture quotations, unless otherwise indicated, are taken from the HOLY BIBLE, NEW INTERNATIONAL VERSION®. NIV®. Copyright © 1973, 1978, 1984 by International Bible Society. Used by permission of Zondervan. All rights reserved.

Scripture quotations marked NKJV are taken from the New King James Version®. Copyright © 1982 by Thomas Nelson, Inc. Used by permission. All rights reserved. *NKJV* is a trademark of Thomas Nelson, Inc.

Library of Congress Cataloging-in-Publication Data

Tomlinson, Loreane.
    LT & me : what raising a champion taught me about life, faith, and listening to your dreams / Loreane Tomlinson with Patti Britton and Ginger Kolbaba.
        p. cm.
    Includes bibliographical references.
    ISBN 978-1-4143-3164-5 (hc)
        1. Tomlinson, LaDainian. 2. Football players—United States. 3. Tomlinson, Loreane. 4. Mothers—United States. 5. Mothers and sons. 6. Faith. I. Britton, Patti M. II. Kolbaba, Ginger. III. Title. IV. Title: LT and me.
    GV939.T65T65 2009
    796.332092—dc22
    [B]   2009010472

Printed in the United States of America

15	14	13	12	11	10	09
7	6	5	4	3	2	1

This book is dedicated to my children:

Londria, my sweet, precious daughter;

LaVar, my wonderful and comical younger son;

and of course LaDainian, my older son, who has been my rock.

And to my grandchildren, who are the apples of my eye.

CONTENTS

By *LaDainian Tomlinson*
With Patti M. Britton

ONE OF MY earliest memories of my mother is her telling me, "You can do it." Now you may wonder what "it" was, and I'll tell you—anything I set my mind to. As I was growing up, she saw that I had a talent and passion for football. She set the wheels turning to do whatever she had to do to make a nine-year-old's dream of going to the NFL come true.

When she looked at me when I was nine and told me that I would be playing in the NFL someday, she must have seen something other people didn't. Because there were people waiting in line to tell me all the reasons this dream would never happen.

But she taught me not to listen to those who were telling me that I couldn't do it. When I did something well, she would praise me. When I hit a slump, she would encourage me. And the times when it seemed like there was an obstacle neither one of us could handle, she prayed me through it. She made me believe that this was going to happen. Once you reach that point, you are halfway there.

But before all of that, she worked to build character in me.

Mom had an endless list of rules that taught me to respect others as well as myself. She didn't accept a shrug as an answer—she told me to use my words. And she instilled a deep faith in all of us and kept us in church. Sometimes breaking those rules carried a stiff penalty, but those lessons have guided me all my life.

When I came home with a brochure about a football camp that I knew was expensive, she used the sweat of her brow to get me there. I learned my work ethic from watching her go to work, and sometimes it was more than one job.

But no matter how tired she was, she sat down with me in the evening and helped me with my homework. Her dedication to my studies may have been what made me return to TCU to complete my degree program after I was in the NFL.

I have always admired and loved my mother. And it was on an occasion that I had disappointed her that I wrote a letter that she still carries with her. In that letter I laid out my goals of going to college, playing ball there, and graduating. Then I wrote that if God was willing, I would go to the NFL. And finally I told her that I wanted to make her the proudest mother in the world. I was determined to do anything I could to restore the pride she had in me. Later I would learn that even when I had let her down, she never stopped loving me or lost her pride in me.

When we talked about her writing this book, I gave her my support and encouragement. Because even though it contains some things that are hard to revisit, I want the world to know how believing in a child can change his life. And I want young men and women who are interested in sports to take hope from my story. Also, I want every father and mother to inspire their children as my mother did me. I know how busy today's parents are, but it takes no more time to praise a child than it does to discourage him.

Finally, I want to send a word to my mother. I want to thank her and tell her how much I have always loved her.

ACKNOWLEDGMENTS

WRITING *LT & Me* has been a bittersweet journey. I have revisited places and people my heart still longs for, and I have examined emotions I thought were long since buried. Looking back, it seems like my life has been a whirlwind, and when I stop to catch my breath, it amazes me what this little country girl has seen and done.

I would like to take a moment to thank the following people for their special contributions to my life and to this project:

To my children, Londria, LaDainian, and LaVar, who have been mentioned throughout the book, you guys are the best, and I am so very proud of each and every one of you!

To my grandkids, you know your Granny thinks you are the greatest bunch of grandkids in the whole wide world!

Stephanie, Terry, Herman Jr., and Flesphia, thanks for staying in my life and being a meaningful part of our family.

Patti Britton, my friend and coauthor, thanks for being so diligent and helping to get this project completed.

Ginger Kolbaba, thanks for being so easy to work with and keeping deadlines and seeing this work through.

Tyndale House Publishers, Jan Long Harris, and the whole staff, thanks for believing in this project and in me.

To Rachel Aydt, thank you for sharing your knowledge and advising us. I'd also like to thank Alan Zucker and Karin DiSanto, both of IMG, and give a special thanks to Irene Perry.

To the rest of my family, those who are still with us and those who have passed on, I thank God for you all. I would not trade you for anything in the world. Thanks for the encouragement.

INTRODUCTION

"OH, NO," I whispered. "Oh, no, no, no. . . ."

Like millions of other football fans, I was glued to my TV set watching the San Diego Chargers and the New England Patriots battle it out in the 2007 AFC Championship Game. A die-hard Chargers fan, I had made it to almost every home game that season. But this game was in Boston, so even though my son LaDainian Tomlinson is the Chargers' starting running back— and the outcome of this all-important game would determine which team would go to the Super Bowl—I was watching the matchup from my home in Fort Worth, Texas.

New England had already won three Super Bowl titles, and we San Diego fans felt it was the Chargers' turn. LaDainian (LT to his fans) often talked about his responsibility to the team. Victory at the Super Bowl was the ultimate goal—and he considered any-thing else a failure.

So I couldn't believe my eyes when, at the beginning of the second quarter, the television cameras suddenly focused on my son limping off the field and taking a seat on the sidelines. Even though he had sustained a knee injury (a sprained medial col-lateral ligament—essentially a small tear) the week before during the divisional round game against the Indianapolis Colts, I had been cautiously optimistic when he took the field just minutes earlier. But now, as he took a seat on the bench, my heart skipped a beat and I sucked in my breath. At that moment, I knew that his injury was more serious than he had been letting on.

If it was possible for him to play through the pain, LT would still be out on the field. He'd been doing that all his life. He'd played with broken ribs, thumbs, arms—you name it. So when I saw my son heading for the sidelines, I knew he was in much bigger trouble than any of us realized. There was simply no way that man would leave the game if he had one more ounce of strength and push in him.

"Oh, no," I whispered again as I watched the television cameras switching back and forth between the plays on the field and LaDainian, number 21, sitting stolidly on the sidelines, his helmet still on, the dark visor that had earned him the nickname "the man behind the mask" firmly in place. "Please, God, You've got to give him Your strength."

The commentators repeatedly discussed LaDainian's departure from the field and how it would affect the outcome of this last play-off game before the Super Bowl. This was supposed to be the year the Chargers were going all the way to the championship game, and LT was going to help them win. Everybody knew it—especially me.

But now LaDainian was sitting on the sidelines. Although he tried to go back on the field one more time, his injury was too intense. LT was out of the game. And as if his injury weren't bad enough, Philip Rivers, their quarterback, had injured both knees, and Antonio Gates, the tight end/wide receiver, had turf toe. The team was in bad shape.

The camera focused on LT again. He sat stone still, not even able to encourage his teammates on the field. It was so unlike him that I knew for sure he really felt helpless.

Tears began to roll down my cheeks. In all the years I had

been a football mom, I'd never seen him like this. His dreams were shattered. Since he was a nine-year-old boy playing Pop Warner youth football in Waco, this was the moment he had aimed for—the moment when he would reach the Super Bowl. Now it was gone as quickly as a mist. And in football, "next year" is never a guarantee.

"Oh, Danian," I whispered as the camera focused in on him again. "Oh, baby, I'm sorry. I'm so, so sorry."

A football player's mother sees the game through different eyes than those of a typical fan. The brutality of the sport seldom leaves our minds. LT says that playing each game is like being in a car wreck. And at the end of each season, his body has suffered the effects of twenty such collisions. Whenever he was a hurt as a child, I could hold him in my arms and comfort him. But in the sports arena, I can only hold him in my heart and prayers.

My tears turned to sobs, and my body shook. I wanted to crawl through that television screen and take him in my arms once again. My son had been through so much. We had been through so much. And I knew, behind that dark visor, he was either crying or close to tears.

I knew my son. A mother always knows her son.

PART ONE

MARLIN, TEXAS

CHAPTER 1

Born to Break Records

LADAINIAN WAS BREAKING records from the time he was born. When I was pregnant with LaDainian in the summer of 1979, I felt as big around as a boat. I was on my feet all day, working at HEB, the local grocery store in my hometown of Marlin, Texas. That was difficult, but I tried to stay healthy and in shape by walking in the evenings and keeping busy. And since this was my second child, I felt pretty confident about what to expect. The birth of my daughter, Londria, had been long, but relatively easy, seven years earlier. And she was a sweet, quiet, gentle child. She slept through the night early on, and I took quickly to being a mother.

My husband, Oliver—whom everybody called Tee—and I talked often about our second child. Tee had asked me early in my pregnancy if I wanted a boy or a girl. Just like every mother, I told him it didn't really matter as long as the baby had ten fingers and ten toes. But deep down, I admit I was hoping for another daughter. I figured another girl would be easier. After all, I would know what to expect because of having Londria. And I didn't know anything about raising boys. They had their own issues!

But Tee shook his head. "No," he said. "This baby needs to be a boy. Every woman should have a son to help her and protect her."

I didn't think much about Tee's words. I was too busy raising our daughter, working to help pay the bills, preparing for the
birth of this new child, and wondering how this second baby
would affect our lives.

June 22 was a typical central Texas day—hot. Temperatures
hovered in the low hundreds. My doctor had marked my due date
for the next day, June 23, so I was feeling anxious and eager about
the baby's arrival. I had a burst of energy that day and cleaned
everything. I didn't feel tired—I couldn't believe it! Later that evening, I took a shower and got ready for bed. Even though the air-
conditioning felt cool, I still couldn't get comfortable. Tee brought
a fan into our bedroom, but even that didn't seem to help.

I finally dozed off to sleep until about one in the morning,
when the baby decided it was time to make an entrance. Jerking
awake from the painful contraction, I thought, *I don't remember
my last labor being this bad.* I immediately woke Tee, because I
figured if I was in pain, he was going to need to be awake to go
through this with me! My bag had been packed a week ago, so
I was ready to go.

"The baby's coming, Tee," I told him.

Tee jumped up, dressed, and ran to get Londria. He got her
settled in the car while I called my mom to alert her that we were
on our way.

Although our small town of Marlin had a hospital, it did not
have a maternity ward. My obstetrician practiced in Marlin but
used the birthing facilities at the hospital in Rosebud, about
twenty miles away. So we dropped Londria off at my mom's
house and set out for Rosebud. I was in so much pain, I wondered if I was going to make the car ride or if I was just going
to pop this baby out during the drive over.

We made it to the hospital, where the staff checked me out
and monitored my contractions.

"Well, Mrs. Tomlinson," the doctor on call finally said, "you still have a long way to go. You're barely dilated. You might as well go back home. We'll see you sometime tomorrow evening."

Tomorrow evening? I thought. *Is this man crazy? Does he not understand the kind of pain I'm in?* I'd had a baby before—I knew hard contractions when I felt them!

Tee placed his arm around me and guided me back out to the car so we could make the twenty-mile drive home again. The pain was overwhelming. I rocked back and forth; I puffed my breath; I did everything I could think of to lessen the pain, but nothing helped.

"Oh, God, just let this be over already!" I prayed out loud. Londria's birth hadn't been this bad. As a matter of fact, I was sure that *no* mother had experienced the labor pains I was experiencing—or for this long! The contractions seemed to go on and on. By about seven that morning, I couldn't take it any longer.

"Tee, we've got to go back to the hospital," I yelled. "*Now!* This baby's killing me!"

Back into the car we went, retracing the twenty miles to Rosebud and into the maternity ward. But we received the same news: "You're not ready to have this baby, Mrs. Tomlinson."

This time Tee shook his head. "Uh-uh. I'm not taking her back. She's hurting too bad. I am *not* taking her back."

I didn't know whether he was supporting me with understanding or if he was sparing himself from having to listen to me moan and wail, but it didn't matter. The doctor agreed and assigned me a room.

Tee was able to stay in the room with me. He was such a big, strong man—in most circumstances. This was not one of them. He looked as if he were in the same amount of pain I was! Every time I groaned, he cringed and looked away.

For the next several hours, I stayed in the room crying and feeling the most intense pain I'd ever experienced. I happened to look over at Tee and saw that he was crying too.

"What are you crying about?" I asked him. I couldn't figure
out why he seemed to be suffering so much. After all, we had
Londria and he had four other children from a previous relationship, so it wasn't as if this labor stuff was new to him. He just
shook his head and wiped his face. I think seeing me in so much
pain was just too difficult for him.

Finally a nurse came in and checked to see how much I
was dilated. Apparently I had hit the magic number, and they
prepped me to go to the delivery room. The best part was
the epidural: the pain eased, and I was a much nicer person
after that!

Tee walked next to me as they wheeled me down the hallway, then he held back slightly as they turned my gurney to
go into the delivery room. But Dr. Phillips placed his hand
on Tee's arm.

"Come on in," he told my husband. "You won't want to
miss this!"

Tee hesitated but slowly followed. I wondered if Tee was going
to need his own medical attention; I was sure he was going to
pass out from the whole ordeal. Men are strong in some things,
but Tee couldn't even stand to see me cry. I didn't know how he
was going to handle childbirth! But I give Tee an E for effort. He
really tried.

Since arriving at the hospital the second time, I had been in
hard labor. At 12:10 p.m. on Saturday, June 23, 1979, almost
twelve hours after my first contractions, our baby was born, our
LaDainian—all nine pounds, three ounces of him.

He'd broken his first record in my book: he gave me the most
difficult labor of the three children I'd have! But somehow I forgot all about that as soon as the nurse placed him in my arms.
Anxiously, I counted his little brown fingers and toes. They were
all there, and I sighed with relief and joy. As I held this precious
baby in my arms and looked into his big, dark chocolate eyes, I

remembered what Tee had told me several months earlier: "Every woman should have a son to help her and protect her."

But I was my son's protector for now. "We're going to have a wonderful life together," I whispered. "I'll get to know you; you get to know me. I'm Mom. Always remember that. And you're my son. Okay?" He gurgled, cried, and flung his tiny hands up and down in response.

I was nervous about having a boy. But somehow I knew this little baby was going to bring joy to our lives. God had blessed us with a special, beautiful child who would change our lives forever.

|||

Back at home in Marlin, I looked forward to returning to a normal routine with my family, but LaDainian had other plans. This was no normal child; he cried night and day.

The longer his crying continued, the more nervous I became. I knew this was the only way a baby could tell his mother something was wrong. So finally, after another long night with no sleep, I settled him into his car seat and headed for the doctor's office.

"He's fine," Dr. Phillips told me. "He just has air in his stomach. That's fairly common for babies. You just need to make sure you burp him really good after you feed him."

"But he cries *all* the time."

"Well, just burp him. I'm sure he'll be fine."

I packed up Dainian and headed home. However, no matter how often I burped him, the crying continued.

Several weeks passed, and he continued to wail. We couldn't take him anywhere because he was so disruptive. I knew he was in misery, and Tee and I were too!

There was nothing we could do to make Dainian settle down. We bought everything available to rock or roll him in, hoping it would help him go to sleep. I sat up all night rocking him, both of us crying.

Tee would take a turn when I couldn't function properly. We even got in the car and drove around at all hours trying to get him to settle down, but nothing worked. I didn't know a baby could cry this much or work himself into such a frenzy as LaDainian did. It was another record! How long could he cry and go without sleep? And how long could Tee and I go without sleep?

When the time came for me to go back to work, I wondered how I was going to leave my baby with someone when he was obviously in such pain. But I *had* to go back to work. So I dropped him off at the nursery and told the staff what was going on. She nodded reassuringly and told me he would be in good hands. They had dealt with these things before.

One day I encountered Mrs. Cheeves, a treasured member of our community who tallied at least one hundred years of living. Out in the country, we took advice from these older women. We respected their age and wisdom, and they knew home remedies that could help—in this case, an elixir that would restore peace and quiet to our home.

"How is that new baby?" she asked me.

I sighed. "I'll just be so glad when we can get a good night's sleep; he cries all the time."

"Well, baby, he's probably colicky."

I said, "Yes, ma'am. So what should I do?"

"Go on over to the drugstore and ask the pharmacist for some asafetida."

"Some what, ma'am?" I couldn't understand what she said. It came out more like "athafethadah," since the poor woman didn't have her teeth in.

"Asafetida," she said again. "Pinch off a little piece, mash it up real fine, mix it with Baby Percy, and put it in the nipple part of his bottle. Let him suck on that a while. That'll settle him."

I wasn't sure what asafetida was. But if it could bring some calm and quiet to our home, I was ready to give her elixir a try. As soon as I got off work, I rushed to the drugstore, made my purchase, picked up the kids from school and day care, and then headed home to care for my colicky baby.

I opened the small bag and just about passed out from the pungent, offensive odor. It made my eyes water; I had never smelled anything so nasty before. I almost shoved it back into the sack and pitched it. But the sounds of LaDainian's wails made me push on. I took a deep breath and held it as I looked at the yellow-brown leaf. *Well, here goes,* I thought, and I did as Mrs. Cheeves had instructed me.

And wouldn't you know it? LaDainian sucked it down, burped easily, and went right to sleep. I kept to that prescription for the next few days, and we never had a problem again. This little boy was having a rough start. I only hoped parenting him would get easier.

|||

Now that LaDainian's crying was under control, Tee, Londria, and I settled into life with a little boy in the house. It was especially fun to watch seven-year-old Londria take to her new brother. She treated LaDainian as though he were *her* baby. She helped feed him, held him, and even changed his diapers. She loved making sure LaDainian was well taken care of.

And Tee enjoyed his son too. I often caught him holding LaDainian and just looking at him. Seeing the two of them together like that always brought a smile to my face.

But early on, I could see that Tee and I had very different parenting styles. With Londria, for some reason, it had not been as noticeable. But once Dainian came along, I began to see our differences rather quickly. The first time it became apparent was when Dainian was around a year and a half old. Convinced that he was ready to move to a sippy cup, I suggested that we throw away the bottle, but Tee disagreed.

"Dainian likes that bottle," he said. "Let him keep it." From the very start, Tee made sure that whatever Dainian wanted, Dainian got.

Not one to be dissuaded, though, I simply threw the bottle away. The next day I discovered Tee had gone out and purchased another. And thus began the bottle wars. I would hide the bottle; Tee would find it and return it to his boy. I would throw it away; Tee would buy another. One day Tee and I entered the kitchen to find an almost-three-year-old LaDainian sitting on the floor by the refrigerator with a gallon jug of milk. He was busily trying to unscrew the lid of his bottle so he could help himself to a refill.

I crossed my arms. "*Now* do you think he is old enough to give up the bottle?" I demanded.

But both Tee and LaDainian were stubborn and persistent. LaDainian refused to drink from a cup, and Tee refused to make him. I feared LaDainian would enter high school and still have his bottle with him!

A few days after Dainian's third birthday, I decided the day had come to end the bottle wars once and for all. It was trash day, and Dainian and I went out to the curb to wait for the garbage truck, bottle in hand.

When the truck arrived, I told Dainian, "Tell the bottle bye-bye," as I tossed the bottle in with the rest of the trash. A small hand raised, waving good-bye. His sad little voice said, "Bye-bye, bottle."

To drive home the point I said, "Now LaDainian, that bottle is in with all the trash. You don't want that back, do you? It's *nasty*." I contorted my face into the most disgusted look I could muster.

"Nasty," echoed the small voice, as he imitated the look on my face. Problem solved.

Unfortunately, that didn't work so well on his father! Though we no longer had the issue with the bottle, we now had another problem to deal with. Dainian seemed to have a sixth sense when it came to knowing what time his father would return home from work. Even as young as three years old, he somehow knew that it was nearing his dad's arrival time. I thought it was so sweet to see my baby boy sitting quietly, watching out the window for his dad's car to pull into our driveway. What I didn't realize, though, was that LaDainian wasn't just waiting for his dad—he was waiting for what his dad brought him every night.

One night as I was brushing Dainian's teeth, I noticed that they weren't the white they should have been. Instead they were covered with little dark spots. I'm not sure how I hadn't noticed it before.

"Tee?" I yelled into the living room, where Tee was sitting. "What's wrong with Dainian's teeth?"

Tee walked in and looked, then shrugged. "I don't know."

I stood up straight and put my hands on my hips. "This boy's teeth look rotten." Somehow I knew Tee had something to do with it. That's when I found out the truth: every night when Tee came home from work, he brought candy for Dainian!

Between sucking on his bottle for so long and eating all that candy—both compliments of his father—Dainian's mouth was a mess. However, Tee didn't seem to be as concerned about the problem as I was.

"Oh, he's all right," was all he said.

That statement became Tee's motto for just about anything that happened to Dainian, and it drove me crazy! Tee always played the role of the laid-back, no-feathers-ruffled, let's-spoil-them parent, while I played the overprotective, stern disciplinarian. The truth was that my children needed both to balance out, something we would discover as our family continued to grow.

CHAPTER 2

Discovering Football

IT SEEMS THAT LaDainian traded in his bottle for a football.

He was about four years old the first time he had a football in his hands. After having a daughter for seven years, Tee and I were excited about buying toys for our first son. But it wasn't long before the train track broke or the car's battery died, and I would hear Dainian say, "Mama, it doesn't work anymore."

Tee and I solved that problem by giving him things that didn't need batteries: balls. We gave him every kind of ball you could imagine—basketballs, baseballs, and of course, footballs. And Dainian loved them all, which thrilled his father. Finally, Tee had someone in the house to share his love of football with.

I had never really been interested in football until Tee and I got married. In high school I attended all the football games, but I was not all that engrossed in the sport; I was in marching band and played trombone and baritone horn. But sports were Tee's life. So I figured either I could be a football widow during football season or I could learn the game and watch it with him. That turned out to be a great decision, since our family spent hours watching and talking about football.

Our favorite team was the Dallas Cowboys. Whenever a game

was on television, we were watching. Almost every Sunday after-noon LaDainian and his dad would sit on the couch together and watch the games. That was their special bonding time. And LaDainian caught on to the game quickly—more quickly than I ever did. If Tee happened to be out of the room and heard the crowd cheering on the television, he would yell, "What hap-pened, LaDainian?"

Four-year-old Dainian would call back, describing the play in detail, including the players' names. My jaw dropped the first time I heard him give a play-by-play with the same level of expertise as the sportscasters. *How is he doing that?* I wondered. I couldn't explain it. He showed a remarkable understanding of the complicated game at a very young age.

We noticed that Dainian had a natural talent for sports: basketball, football, any kind of ball—it didn't matter. Since Londria's friends were always up for a quick game of football or baseball, Dainian developed his skills by playing with the older kids. This gave him the advantage when he played against kids his own age. It seemed as though Dainian was always chal-lenging someone to some kind of contest. I would often hear him say, "Let's race" or "Let's see if I can hit the ball farther than you."

Even at his young age, it was as though he understood the importance of discipline and perseverance. For his fifth birthday, Dainian wanted a "big boy" bike—without train-ing wheels. As usual, if Dainian wanted something, Tee made sure he had it. Dainian was so excited when he received the bike, and he immediately wanted to go out and learn to ride it. "This is a big bike. I'm a big boy," he told us, looking very serious.

We told him we would teach him as soon as we finished our chores around the house. Knowing we could depend on our responsible LaDainian not to go in the street, I wasn't alarmed when I heard him slip out the front door. I figured he would play until we could teach him.

As soon as I finished cleaning the house, I walked outside to find an obviously injured LaDainian crying.

"What happened?" I asked, now feeling nervous about this new gift.

"He's all right," called our neighbor, a former schoolteacher, from across the street. "He's been doing that for thirty minutes. Falling, crying, and getting up. He ran into a tree a while ago and bumped his head."

"Why didn't you call me?" I asked.

"Because he's all right," she answered nonchalantly. "He has more tenacity than any young man I've ever known."

The definition of tenacity is this: "tending to hold firmly; persistent." That describes my son. He was set to conquer that bike without the training wheels. And he learned to ride by never giving up. He never went into the street to do it, either. We didn't have sidewalks, so all of that falling and getting up had taken place in the front yard. It's difficult enough to learn to ride a bicycle on concrete. It's next to impossible to learn on grass, but LaDainian did.

As he grew, I kept noticing his tenacity, his joy of being outdoors and running, and his knowledge of all things about football, from statistics to plays to players. But he still amazed and surprised me when, at six years old, he asked Tee and me for a weight set for Christmas.

Tee and I didn't know whether it was appropriate for a six-year-old to have the weights, but after we talked it over, we figured if he had the nerve to ask for them, we would give them to him. We just could not get over how serious our son was about strengthening his body. Our main concern was that he would take on more than he could handle.

Even though it would be another three years before he

actually began to play organized sports, it seemed he knew at that tender age that he was meant to be an athlete. He was very mindful of his body, what he put into it, and how he treated it. Little did we truly understand that this was a discipline he would carry throughout the rest of his life.

CHAPTER 3

Small-Town Life

MARLIN, TEXAS, was a great place to raise a family. When I was growing up, Marlin was a sleepy little town of about nine thousand people. The town made its mark on the map as the official "Mineral Water City of Texas." These waters were supposed to cure everything from acne to arthritis.

At one time in its history, Marlin was a thriving town with people coming from all over to partake of and soak in these special waters. But by the time my kids were born, Marlin was just another small town—a good, safe place to grow up, where everybody knew everybody and watched out for one another.

When you live in a small town, life just seems simpler. The smallest things, like a cool breeze, freshly baked cookies, or lightning bugs, brought us pleasure. The surrounding countryside was perfect for anything we wanted to do. We could relax under a giant oak tree, hunt in the woods outside of town, or sit on the creek bank and fish.

Our family loved to fish. I was off one day, so I piled my kids and some of the neighborhood children into our station wagon. We bought a bunch of fifty-nine-cent cane poles and headed to the creek a few miles outside of town. I showed them how to fish, and LaDainian took to it like a fish takes to water! He was the first to catch one and ended up doing the best of all of us that day.

That boy loved being outside. That's where he spent most of his time, whether it was fishing, riding his bike, or playing with his friends. All Tee and I asked was that he and his brother and sister be home before dark. We felt they would be safe, because in our community, adults were mother and father to every child— whether that child was theirs or not. If a neighbor saw one of our children misbehaving, he or she might give that child a swat and tell us about it. We were thankful for that, and we did the same for their children.

Having the protection from our community made life easier because Tee and I worked hard, sometimes two or three jobs at a time, to make ends meet. That meant that from the time our children were six weeks old, they were in the nursery. I wasn't thrilled about being away from them, but we knew everybody in town, so we knew we could trust the child care staff to watch and protect our kids.

For the most part we didn't have trouble with the kids in child care—except for the fact that LaDainian was a little biter. His teacher often called me and said, "Mrs. Tomlinson, your son is biting the other kids *again.*" I didn't know what to do, and I told the teacher I was at a loss. Finally, after several calls, I asked Tee about it.

"Oh, yeah, my other kids were biters too," he told me. "Instead of hitting or pushing like other children do, they bit."

"Well, how did you handle that?"

"We bit them back."

So I gave those instructions to the teacher.

"Mrs. Tomlinson," she told me, sounding shocked. "We can't have our teachers or children biting your son back."

"Well, then call me," I told her. "I'll come and bite him, because my children are not getting kicked out of day care."

One day one of the kids did bite LaDainian back, and that was the end of his biting. He must have figured if one child bit him, the others might too.

That was really the only trouble we had with LaDainian. For the most part, I never had to worry about him. He was a good little boy. He did what he was told and was very protective of his family. They loved playing with the other kids there. LaDainian especially liked being an older brother to LaVar and watching out for him. He took the role of older brother and eldest son seriously, even at that young age.

There was one time, however, when LaDainian took his big-brother responsibilities a bit too far. LaVar was still a baby, and I dropped the boys off at day care. LaVar had developed an ear infection, which began to cause him considerable pain as the day wore on.

The day care worker called to let me know that LaVar had a slight temperature and that she would keep an eye on him. But later in the day, LaVar began to cry more persistently.

When the day care worker didn't respond to LaVar's cries right away, Dainian went straight to her, tugged on her skirt, and said, "My baby is crying."

"I'll be right there, LaDainian," the worker told him. "Go wait for me by his crib, okay?"

When Dainian got to his brother's crib, he noticed that pus was trickling out of LaVar's ears. So LaDainian took matters into his own hands. He found a cotton swab and began to dig in LaVar's ears to clean them. The day care worker rushed over in a panic, afraid that LaDainian was going to burst LaVar's eardrum. She got everything back under control and called me.

Even though it looked bad with the pus coming out of LaVar's ears, the doctor informed us that this wasn't unusual and gave us some medication that cleared it up. Fortunately, LaDainian's medical career ended right there. At least he meant well.

|||

It was important to us to provide our children with the things we
never had growing up. Our children were rich compared to what
my childhood had been like.

My first home in Marlin was a small, two-room frame house
that seven of us—my parents, four siblings, and I—shared. One
room was the kitchen; the other served as the living room during
the day and our bedroom at night.

When I was five years old, my parents built a six-room house
that had a living area, a kitchen, three bedrooms, and a screened-
in porch. Although it was more spacious than our previous home
and we were able to spread out, the conditions were still primi-
tive. In the winter we depended on a wood-burning stove in the
living room to keep us warm. And in the summer, when the sun
beat down on the little house, we had to rely on Mother Nature
to send a breeze our way. Unfortunately, it seemed that in August
she saved her breath. At night during the summer, we kids—
Theopal, Ike, Bertha, Mary, and I—would pull our mattresses out
to the screened-in porch to sleep and escape the heat.

We had no running water in the house, so we had big barrels
of water delivered to use for drinking, cooking, and washing. No
running water also meant no indoor plumbing or bathroom. So
we used an outhouse located toward the edge of our backyard. In
the evenings, Mom would make all five children take one last trip
there together before bed.

Most houses in our area had big barrels of water sitting by
them like ours did, but not my aunt's house. She was rich. She
had a well that used an electric pump to pull out her water. We
were always so amazed by that pump.

My family worked hard to have the things we did. During
late spring and summer, a truck would come into our neighborhood early in the morning to pick us up and take us out to

work in the fields. Until sundown, my brother and sisters and I would join my dad and mom and other families out in the fields helping to chop and pull cotton. We didn't have gloves, so our hands were calloused. We didn't have shade, either—and those summer days were hot! We would spend all day in eighty- to one hundred–degree weather. And when we went home, we didn't enter an air-conditioned house. When it was hot, it was hot everywhere!

After we finished working, we were ready to go outside and play, so we played while my mom and dad cooked our supper. Then we would bathe in a big laundry tub. Because water was valuable, all five of us kids used the same water, maybe only changing the water once. Once we were cleaned up, we were ready to go back outside and play again, but we weren't allowed to since we might get dirty.

I was a tomboy, and I always wanted to hang out with my dad. With five kids to take care of, my dad worked long and hard. So getting personal attention from him was difficult. I figured if I hung out around him and helped him work, then I could con- nect with him. We call that "bonding" today. It didn't matter what the work was, I was there—chopping wood, repairing the chicken coop, or building a fence. I enjoyed that time. My dad never said much as I worked beside him. But it didn't matter. It was just being with him that was so special.

Even though the work was hard, life was simple. We rose at dawn, worked or went to school, played, did our chores, went to church faithfully, and spent time with family. Looking back, I realize we were dirt poor, but as a child I thought we lived in the Garden of Eden. And actually we lived a lot healthier than many families do today. All of our food was "organic." We had fruit trees everywhere: plums, peaches, figs, persimmons, and dates. We harvested the wild blackberries from bushes around our house, and my mom would bake them in cobblers.

No one ever heard of childhood obesity because we got plenty of exercise. We didn't have a car, so we walked or ran everywhere. And without toys or television, we were very inventive in our playing. In the evenings, after our chores were done, all the children in the neighborhood would gather outside to run races or play hopscotch, hide-and-seek, and pop the whip. Pop the whip was one of my favorite games. We would hold hands and form a long line, then we would run and bend our bodies until we created such momentum that the person at the end of the line was lifted off the ground.

When we weren't playing, we helped the neighbors with different chores. We never got paid; it was just to give us something to do. One of our neighbors had cows and chickens, so we often went to her house and helped her collect the eggs from her henhouse or churn butter.

I never felt poor or deprived, because everyone in our area lived the same way. We didn't own a television for a long time, so we never saw how other people lived. We just thought we were normal—that everybody lived the way we did.

That began to change when I entered the fifth grade. That year our school combined with the school on the other side of town. Those children were different. Whenever I walked past them, they pointed at me and laughed. I asked my sisters what those kids thought was so funny.

As time passed I began to understand why they laughed. I heard them call us poor, though I didn't even know what the word meant. It became clear, though, when the Christmas holidays came around.

One day after our Christmas break, a girl with fancy clothes asked me what I got for Christmas. I told her I got the dress I was wearing.

"That old thing?" she said and laughed. Her words cut deep. I knew the dress was used, but that had never mattered before. I had been excited about receiving clothes. Usually our Christmas presents consisted of fruit—grapefruit, oranges, and apples. Only on really special Christmases did we receive clothing or shoes. And one Christmas I received a bald-headed boy baby doll that I treasured! Now this little girl was making fun of what I considered a special Christmas present. It was painful.

Then Valentine's Day arrived. We had never even heard of Valentine's Day, and we couldn't afford to give out cards. I must have looked so crazy that day, because when I received cards from my classmates, I ogled them, openmouthed, and held them tenderly. While the other children probably threw their valentines away a day or two later, I cherished and saved mine for a long time. I had never seen anything like them in my life.

Life really changed for us when I turned sixteen. I was the oldest child still at home. Theopal and Ike were both out on their own, so it was my parents, me, Bertha, and Mary left in the house. That summer I went to visit my aunt in Houston. She was a teacher but worked as a house sitter during the summers.

On July 21, I got a call from my sister Bertha, who was days away from turning fourteen. I could tell immediately something was wrong. Her voice was trembling.

"Daddy's dead," she burst out and started to cry.

I couldn't believe it. "No! Why? How?"

We were all in shock.

Bertha told me our father had had a stroke. They rushed him to the hospital, but he died.

I didn't know how we were going to go on. I just had no idea how much his death would truly change our lives. He left us, especially my mother, unprepared to cope. My mom had been sheltered. My dad did almost everything. He did most of the cooking, not because my mom didn't cook; she *couldn't* cook—her cooking was terrible. So Dad cooked. He also shopped and paid all the bills. When he died, my mom didn't know how to do anything! She didn't know how to shop for us or how to deal with finances. Now she had to figure out how to support her family. She tried to keep us from worrying about our situation because she didn't think children should have to worry about "grown-up problems."

She would often say, "Don't you worry. The good Lord will provide." But I wasn't so sure. I believed in God and I dutifully attended church with my family. But I often sat in the service and wondered, *Is this all there is to God? There has to be more than this.* As I wondered how a good God could allow my mother and family such pain, life went from bad to worse.

I always believed in God, but I didn't really understand the idea of having a personal relationship with Him—that we could go to Him with all our concerns and needs, and that He would be there to walk with us through those trials.

One day my mother gathered my sisters and me around her and told us, "We've got to move." We had gotten behind on the house payments, so the bank took the house and we had to find another place to live. Leaving the property we had grown up on was heartbreaking, even though we were fortunate to find another house.

Mom knew she had to find work, but her health wasn't that good—she had congestive heart failure. Besides, living in a small town afforded few job opportunities. A cousin had a job at the local turkey factory in town and suggested that my mother apply for work there. My mom tried it, but she lasted only one day. When she came home, her clothes were covered with turkey blood, and she was in intense pain from her swollen feet and legs. They were so bloated I thought they would pop. Being on her feet all day was simply too much; she could not stand for long periods of time.

So my brother, sisters, and I had to step up and supplement the small amount of social security our mother received. My older sister and brother sent money home. But Bertha, Mary, and I were still in school, so we couldn't help too much with the finances. Instead, we did our best to help with the chores around the house. During the summer, I found a job at the Veterans Administration in Marlin. Later I worked long, hard hours at the turkey factory.

I didn't know how we were going to survive. My childhood was gone, and in its place came heavy adult responsibility. In a sense, I guess we all grew up together, my mother and us. I dearly loved my mother. But as I dealt with so much loss and hard work and pain, I determined that I would *never* allow myself to be in a position where I was unable to support myself or my children.

|||

Before I knew it, I had finished high school. Seventeen and recently graduated, I was ready to find out what life held for me. A friend, Jean, and I got jobs at a sewing plant in Waco, about thirty miles away. I knew I wanted to go to college, but I couldn't right away, since my mom and sisters needed my salary to help us live. I turned eighteen in July and figured I would work for a while longer, then go on to college in a year or two.

One swelteringly hot day in the early fall, I headed over to Strickland's, the town café. I was at the counter ordering when my sister Theopal's friend Tommy approached me.

"Say, Loreane," he said, "come on over to the table when you get done here. There's someone I want you to meet."

I glanced at the table he'd pointed to. Sitting with his profile to me was a boy I didn't recognize. So when my order came up, I joined Tommy and his friend, a boy of medium height and build. He smiled wide—a big, beautiful smile that covered his whole face. I was hooked.

"Loreane," Tommy told me, "I want you to meet Oliver 'Tee' Tomlinson."

"Nice to meet you, Oliver," I said in my friendliest voice.

"Tee," he answered. "Everybody calls me Tee."

"Well, it's nice to meet you, Tee," I said. "You from around here?"

"I'm from over on Tomlinson Hill," he said.

I had heard of Tomlinson Hill—it was about seven miles outside of Marlin, on the other side of the Brazos River. It was a tiny community of families. But even still, I thought I knew *everybody* in our area, so I was surprised that I was meeting somebody I didn't know. And somebody as attractive as this man was—how had I possibly missed him?

We fell easily into conversation. And when Tommy suggested we head to the Falls, I quickly agreed. The Falls—interestingly named, since there are no falls there—is a beautiful spot on the Brazos River where people go to fish, swim, camp, have picnics, and just hang out. The three of us played like children, splashing, wading, and laughing. For the first time in two years, I felt young and free again. It was wonderful, a godsend, and it was all because of Tee.

That day at the Falls was just the start of something much bigger between Tee and me. Our attraction to each other was electric. And we tried to spend as much time together as we could.

I was so caught up with him—his charm, his smile, his personality, his masculinity, his hardworking character—that I was completely surprised when he finally confessed that he was thirty-five years old. Seventeen years my senior. I couldn't believe it. He looked and acted my age—so youthful and full of energy. I had just assumed that I didn't know him because he had been away at college.

But after really thinking through the age difference, I decided it did not matter. After all, my father had been thirty years older than my mother.

The real shocker, though, was that Tee had four children

from a previous relationship. At first I thought, *Okay, he has children.* But it didn't sink in, since I had never met them. They didn't seem real. Their mother had moved to Waco after her relationship wiht Tee had ended, and she'd taken the kids with her. Although he told me stories about them and I saw their photos, as long as I didn't see them, they didn't seem to exist. For some reason, I just never thought they were part of his life. Plus it was difficult to think that this man I had fallen in love with had children, one of whom was just a few years younger than I was!

But when I finally met Terry, Ronald, Charles, and Flesphia, I realized they were *very* real. I immediately loved his children, especially Fi-Fi, as we called her. Fi, Ronald, and Charles lived with their mother in Waco. And Terry stayed with Mother Julie, Tee's mom. We didn't see them too often, mostly because they were all involved in sports and other school events.

After about a year of dating, Tee asked me, "How do you feel about marriage?" Although I knew I wanted to get married and have a family someday, I still felt confused about marrying Tee. Even though I liked his children, I wasn't sure I was ready to be the stepmother to four kids. I already had a lot on my plate taking care of my own mother.

But on the other hand, I couldn't imagine my life without Tee. He was outgoing and made me feel special. We had similar faith backgrounds. He had the most wonderful, big smile. He could light up a room within seconds of entering it. He could charm anybody. My mother adored him because he could always make her laugh. One of the most generous men I ever knew, Tee would give someone the shirt off his back or his last dollar. He was a good-hearted person. And he was a hard worker. I think that was part of what drew me to him. He reminded me of my father. In a way, Tee filled some of that loss I had felt since my dad died.

So at the age of nineteen, on February 2, 1972, I traveled with Tee to the neighboring town of Lott, Texas, where the justice of the peace married us. As I looked at this strong, charming, energetic man, I knew Tee and I would have a wonderful life and a wonderful family together.

CHAPTER 4

The Hill

BEFORE TEE AND I GOT MARRIED, Tee had lived on Tomlinson Hill, a tight-knit community of about a hundred people, which was across the Brazos River and about seven miles from Marlin. The area was named after James K. Tomlinson, who had settled there with his slaves back in the 1800s. Many of Tee's family still lived there, including his mom, Mother Julie. Tee owned a one-story white house around the corner and down the sandy road from where she lived.

The first time Tee took me to the Hill, I was quickly enchanted. I could see why Tee loved his hill so much. It was peaceful and quiet and filled with family.

If you looked into Tee's soul, you could tell that his family was the first and foremost thing he cared about. And by family, I don't just mean the children and me and his mother. His definition of family included anybody who lived on the Hill, whether they were related to him by blood or not. On the Hill, there were no strangers to Tee.

When we were first married, we lived in his house on the Hill, and Tee's mother and relatives were always ready to lend a hand. Tee often stopped by his mom's after work to check on her, and many times she would fill his arms with extra food to bring home for our dinner. But we eventually moved back to Marlin because we needed to be close to Londria's day care. Although we remained in Marlin after I had LaDainian and LaVar, we visited Tomlinson Hill often.

It was difficult for Tee to be away from his beloved Hill. If he could have, he would have spent all his time there. It was where he felt the most at ease and free to be himself. Every time we left that place after a visit, Tee's whole demeanor took on a slightly sad look.

Tee and I had a good marriage. We were in love and laughed a lot. Even in my happiest moments, though, I knew Tee had another love: Tomlinson Hill.

Making a living and raising a family took a toll on my husband. My drive to survive had been fueled by seeing my widowed mother be unprepared to carry on without her husband. My oath that this would not happen to me made me take the reins in the family. Like a horse with blinders on, I pushed forward without distraction so I could offer a better life and more opportunities for my children. My first duty was to my children's future, even if it meant working instead of playing.

And Tee could take only so much. I would lay all our problems at his feet, and soon his temptress, the Hill, would whisper in his ear and steal his attention from me. And when this love called, he had to go. Eventually, I came to realize that there was nothing I could do to compete with or change his feelings about the Hill.

Within that world were the people who understood him best: his family. When his mom took him in her arms and locked him in her embrace, I could see his childlike enthusiasm for life return.

Sometimes he simply announced that he was going to the Hill on his own. Since he still owned his house there, I was never sure when he would return home. It could be later that day or in two days. Mostly, though, he wanted us to experience life on the Hill with him. When the stress of daily life got to be too much for us, Tee would say, "Let's go across the river" or "We're going to the Hill," and we would escape to Tee's paradise. He couldn't understand why anyone would want more than this. This piece of land embodied everything he held dear. He would load us all into the car, and as we crossed the river, I always felt as though we were traveling back in time.

Sometimes we would take the back roads to get there. And on the way Tee would announce, "I have a taste for rabbit." As we drove along, I could tell he was searching for one of those small animals. We'd trek over dirt roads covered with brush and trees. Actually, we couldn't really call them roads. We were just driving out in the middle of nothing: no houses anywhere, no pavement—just a few cows grazing.

Tee always kept his rifle in the car—it was legal back then. If he saw a rabbit or squirrel, he would park and pull his gun out of the trunk. While I stayed in the car with the kids, Tee would disappear into a field or the woods. About ten minutes later, we'd hear a shot. Then he would reappear with his prize in hand. He would place the animal in a bag and put it and the rifle in the trunk, and we'd continue our trip to the Hill.

I could see the stress and tension of the world melt away from Tee the closer we got. Troubles, bills, job problems— nothing seemed to reach him while he was there. As soon as we arrived, Tee would skin the animal and hand it over to Mother Julie, who would spend the day cooking it with gravy and rice or potatoes.

Those were special times. These outings were magical for our children as well. Granny always baked something special for them—cookies, cupcakes, or pies. Her house was never without some sort of home-baked goody. As soon as our car pulled onto the Hill, LaDainian was out the door, running to greet his granny, munch on some of her delicious treats, and then head off to find a cousin or two.

LaDainian, LaVar, and Londria loved to go barefoot and feel the warm sand between their toes. And they especially loved to play with their cousins. They had so many cousins that it was difficult to count them all. There always seemed to be something to keep the kids busy on the Hill. Races, hide-and-seek, sports—some kind of game was always going on. I never heard any of my children whine about being bored while they were on the Hill.

LaDainian especially loved playing with the animals in the area. Part of life on the Hill was raising hogs. When we slaughtered a hog, the whole family came to help, and everyone left with meat.

One time when the hogs had a litter, LaDainian decided he wanted one as a pet. He picked out a black and white pig and named it Piglet. He loved that animal. Every time I saw Dainian, I saw Piglet. He constantly held it, petted it, and chased it. That pig was fast—but so was Dainian!

I never could understand why he wanted a pig as a pet. Pigs lie around in filth, urinate in their food and water, and are just plain nasty. I tried to discourage LaDainian from getting too attached to the pig and explained why his attachment would lead only to heartache, since one day that animal was going to become food for us. But Dainian didn't seem to care—or maybe he just didn't believe us.

Eventually the day came when Piglet did, in fact, become our next meal. Of course we didn't let LaDainian know beforehand, because we knew he would try to talk us out of it. When he found out, he was inconsolable. He cried and cried. It broke my heart to see his pain. But food is food.

I understood how he felt. When I was a child, my sisters, brother, and I often named our chickens. I could still remember my dad sitting on the porch with his rifle across his knees, watching to make sure the chicken hawks didn't swoop down out of the sky to steal a chicken. That wasn't because my dad was being thoughtful to the chickens. It was to make sure that the chicken hawks didn't steal our food. Unfortunately, we never knew when our "pet" chickens would end up in a pot with home-made dumplings. But it was guaranteed that they *would*!

Poor thing, I thought as I watched Dainian. After that, he never wanted another pig for a pet again. He was satisfied with dogs—animals that aren't food sources!

LaDainian's favorite times on the Hill came every summer when Tee hosted the family reunion weekend. For days before the reunion, the men constructed massive outdoor tables and benches. The women busied themselves cooking recipes that had been handed down for generations.

And in the center of the whirlwind were Tee and his sidekick, Dainian, feeling the excitement grow as each day passed. Tee became the master of ceremonies as he manned the barbecue pit. The aroma of roasting meat mingled with the scent of wild honeysuckle was intoxicating. Tee insisted that everyone in shouting distance make a plate and eat until they were ready to burst. And Dainian was there watching his father work, energized by his family surrounding him.

During the day we busily occupied ourselves with work and light conversation. At night, we sat around a bonfire under the starry sky and the mesquite trees and reminisced about how life used to be. I got after Dainian all the time about getting too close to the fire. He loved to place a toy on the edge of the fire, then try to grab it before it was engulfed in the flames.

Tomlinson Hill was definitely a magical place—a getaway from the stresses of life and a place for my kids to know and be surrounded by the most important thing in life: family.

CHAPTER 5

Daddy Tee

LADAINIAN HAD A SPECIAL BOND with his father. Dainian was in awe of him. Every time he accomplished anything, he wanted his dad to be the first to know—from catching his first fish to throwing his first football.

Tee loved it. As laid back as Tee was, he still wanted to make sure he instilled values and morals into his children. A master of oral history, Tee often gathered his kids around him and told them the stories of their ancestors. He reminded them that this history was as much a part of them as breathing.

One day I came home from work to find Dainian sitting on the floor listening to one of his father's tales. Tee told Dainian that when Tee was younger, he and his older brother got into a fight. Things escalated, and his brother pulled a knife to get Tee to back down. In the scuffle, two of Tee's fingers were so badly cut that he had to be taken to the doctor. His pinkie and ring fingers were damaged. After examining them, the doctor told Tee he had a choice: the doctor could repair the fingers so they would perma-nently stick straight out, or he could fix them so they would be permanently bent at the knuckle in a fist-like position. Tee chose the latter so he could make a fist to box, another of his favorite sports. With those two fingers already bent in that position, he figured he would be halfway there.

He ended this story with a warning: "Never lose control of your temper, Dainian. Never let your anger get the best of you. Things can quickly get out of hand and become dangerous. You make sure you think about the consequences of your actions." And with that, Tee lifted his bent hand as a reminder of this lesson.

He also continually reminded LaDainian of the importance of his role as the oldest son. "You need to protect your mother, sister, and brother," he told LaDainian. And LaDainian always listened seriously and nodded.

Then he would tell LaDainian and LaVar, "You're brothers. There will come a time in your life when you will go through difficulties, and only your brother will know the things you've gone through, because you have lived with each other and grown up together. So always remember that. Always protect each other. Always honor each other. Always take care of and watch out for each other."

As a mom, I don't think I ever would have put that responsibility on them, but as a father, Tee felt that it was important. I often overheard him telling the boys, "Always mind your mom. She's hard, but mind your mom." Fortunately, that was never something we had a big problem with, since they were not disobedient kids. But I think it was something he felt he had to say.

|||

Tee and I both agreed that we wanted our children, even at a young age, to understand respect and the importance of honoring adults. He made them speak respectfully to their elders, saying, "Yes, ma'am" or "No, ma'am" and "thank you" and "please."

But Tee didn't ride them all the time. Mostly he just liked

to play with his kids. He had an unbelievable amount of energy. He hit the floor running in the mornings, and when he returned from work in the evenings he was ready to play. After supper I could always find Tee and LaDainian out in the yard playing catch.

An avid sportsman, Tee enjoyed baseball and basketball, and he loved to box. He was always ready to play a game of catch or challenge LaDainian to a race. It didn't matter how little my son was, Tee showed him no mercy in their races. Tee held the belief that people become better only by putting themselves up against someone bigger and stronger. And to my knowledge, Tee was one of the few people who could beat Dainian in a race.

Dainian took that practice to heart. Whenever he wanted to race, he looked for someone who would present the greatest challenge to him, someone who would force him to stretch himself.

Tee passed on other values to our children without ever having to say a word. One was the importance of helping around the house. He helped our children understand that real men help around the house. There isn't a gender-specific role in maintaining a home; each person needs to see what has to be done and then do it.

Tee often shared the cooking responsibilities, which of course, I loved. Our favorite times together were Saturday and Sunday mornings when we gathered as a family over breakfast. Tee and I would make ham, sausage, or bacon, and eggs, pancakes, biscuits, and grits. Then the whole family would sit and eat and talk and laugh.

LaDainian often stood in the kitchen and watched his father cook. He loved cookies—so much that we nicknamed him the "cookie monster." He was always asking Tee or me to make him cookies, but when my son's love of cookies exceeded my energy level, I decided it was time to teach him how to do it himself. I didn't understand how much of an impression watching his dad cook had made on him until that day. He never had to deal with the notion that real men don't cook. His dad did, and that was good enough for him. Now all I had to do was keep the ingredients on hand so he could make the chocolate chip cookies he dearly loved. And of course, everybody in the house appreciated Dainian's baking skills!

Although I loved the fact that Tee enjoyed being involved with the kids, I was often frustrated when he didn't take an active role in disciplining them. That role fell on me. Even though I grew weary of always feeling like I was being the bad guy, I wasn't about to give it up. I didn't want to raise a bunch of delinquents and menaces to society. So it was up to me to make sure that didn't happen.

To give him credit, though, Tee did balance my overly protective nature, and at times his laid-back nature was even a blessing. I am a fix-it person. But when it comes to my children, if there's blood involved I fall apart.

During one of our Tomlinson family reunions, LaDainian had challenged his cousin Carl to a race. He was full of adrenaline and headed for victory when he slammed into a hidden barbed wire fence. The wire sliced into his face around his eye and nose. And there was blood everywhere.

I went into panic mode as soon as I saw him running toward me. I was horrified; I didn't know if the wire had sliced into his eye. Had he been blinded? Would he lose his eye? I was shaking and nearly hysterical.

As he walked toward the scene, Tee said calmly, "He's all right."

Irritation immediately filled my body at those words that seemed to be my husband's motto: *He's all right.* My baby was bleeding all over the place. How could he possibly know Dainian was all right?

Tee pushed me out of the way and moved in. "Let me see," he said, pulling a handkerchief from his back pocket.

He bent down and cleaned up the bloody area.

"Oh, it's not that bad," he said, turning back to me. "It just seems bad because it's in an area that can bleed a lot. It's above his eye, but his eye is okay."

His words made sense to me. But I kept trying to peek over his shoulder. "Well, let me see!"

And he was right. He was just the right, sound person for that situation.

Tee cleaned LaDainian up, then he patted his son and sent him off to play again.

I just shook my head. *God help me. Girls are so much easier,* I thought.

I looked at Tee again, who had now gone back to enjoying his family. His smile covered his face. That big smile that lit up the world and made you think everything *was* all right. Every time he flashed me that smile, I thought of how much I loved him. LaDainian inherited that smile.

PART TWO

WACO, TEXAS

CHAPTER 6

The Accident

OURS WAS A STRONG FAMILY. We loved spending time together. The kids adored their father, and he adored them. It seemed as if nothing could destroy the happiness I felt during those years. I had three beautiful, healthy children and my husband, Tee, who was always ready to have a good time. But life is unpredictable, and it's impossible to know where the next step will lead or how one moment can change things forever.

Tee and I had begun to notice that Marlin was changing. One house separated our home from the "mom and pop" grocery store on the corner. This once friendly place was now surrounded by unemployed men and teenagers who were loitering and drinking. The dependable turkey plant periodically shut down, and work was scarce. Teenagers were bored, and there was little opportunity for them to do anything constructive. Street drugs were now making an appearance.

We wanted more than this for our children. So after much discussion, we decided to pack up, leave our extended family, and move thirty miles north to Waco, which was a larger town that offered more opportunities for our children.

We found a small but comfortable house with a yard for the kids to play in. LaDainian, who was about six, and LaVar were still too young to be affected by the move. We had to pull Londria out of junior high, which we felt terrible about, but she also seemed to adjust to the new adventure.

We settled in and enjoyed our life in Waco. But then one day in April 1986, while Tee was working at his job as a roofer for Ridgeland Mobile Homes, he had a terrible accident. He was roofing atop a mobile home when the roof collapsed. He crashed through to the floor, twelve feet below.

Immediately one of his coworkers drove him to the hospital. After the doctor took an X-ray and ran some tests, he informed my husband that he would be okay. The doctor prescribed pain medication and sent him home, telling him to take it easy for a while.

But the pain didn't subside, and Tee didn't seem to be healing. He couldn't work; he couldn't do much of anything. The next few months became an endless blur of doctor's appointments, workers' compensation paperwork, and pain pills. Although he attempted to go back to his job several times, Tee couldn't cope with the intense discomfort and always ended up back at home on the couch.

Finally, about six months later, Tee visited a specialist who ran more tests and discovered that the damage to Tee's back was more severe than they had initially thought. He was going to need surgery.

Doctors removed two discs from his back. His recovery was filled with hours of physical therapy and more painkillers. Still, he was not getting better. The pain and inability to lead a normal life began to take its toll on Tee, and he fell into a deep depression.

His left leg began to give out without warning, and he would have to grab on to something solid to keep from falling. So at his next appointment, he told the doctor about his condition. The doctor ordered more X-rays and, after examining them, told

Tee he would need to use a cane in order to walk. That was devastating to Tee. It was too constricting. How was he supposed to
run races and play ball with Dainian? How would he do simple
things like hunt or fish or walk the roads of his beloved Hill? This
once active man now found himself alone in the house for hours
on end, depressed and in pain.

Tee routinely had checkups about every six weeks. During one
recheck at the doctor's office, the doctor discovered another problem with a disc. This time it was a disc in Tee's neck that needed
to be removed. So the doctor suggested another surgery. But Tee
said no. He wasn't willing to endure another operation.

"If you don't have this operation," the doctor told Tee, "then
there is a good chance that this condition and the pain that
comes with it will stay with you for the rest of your life."

But Tee would not budge from his decision.

I had great compassion for the pain Tee was in. And I could
understand the depression. What I couldn't understand was the
parade of "friends" who started to come around the house while
I was gone. Life in our home became stormy as Tee and I fought
over his behavior. I knew something was going on that wasn't
right, but he kept denying that he was doing anything illegal or
detrimental to our family.

I didn't know what exactly was going on, but I did know that
Tee was acting strange. He became jittery and forgetful. I could
blame some of it on the depression and the medication. His
blood pressure had spiked—I supposed from the pain. So he was
on blood pressure medication and an aspirin routine as well as
the pain medication. But his behavior wasn't making sense to me.

Right after his accident, Tee had tried hard to make sure the
children never saw him in pain. Although it took a physical
toll on him, he still tried to be an active father. But even that
had begun to change, and the children started to ask questions.
LaVar was preschool age, so he didn't know anything was wrong.

Although Londria and LaDainian were still young enough not to understand fully, they knew something wasn't right with their dad. Londria, especially, started to ask me, "What's wrong with Daddy? He's acting strange."

I could only answer that their dad was in pain and the pain made him act that way.

But I also began to hear strange comments from other people. Since Waco is so close to Marlin, we continued to go to church there and visited family and friends whenever we could. Everybody knew Tee, and I began to run into people who would say, "I saw Tee the other day. He didn't look the same. Is he okay?"

"He's been going through some things since he had the accident," I'd explain. I felt uncomfortable answering them, though, because deep down I knew something wasn't right with him. I just didn't know what to say, and I wasn't sure I really wanted to think about it.

I tried to pray about our situation, seeking wisdom, but even though we still attended church, I had fallen away some from my faith. My church taught us that God was a judge who didn't really concern Himself with the everyday matters of our lives. Although I believed in God, He wasn't a real power in my life, and when I would pray, I didn't feel any comfort or any answers.

One day I returned home early from work. I walked in the house and found a jittery, nervous Tee with a man I had never seen before.

"What's going on here?" I demanded.

"Nothing, nothing," replied Tee. But I could tell something was wrong with him.

I turned to the stranger and yelled, "You get out of my home!" Then I turned back to Tee and looked him straight in the eyes. "If anything like this ever happens again, you can pack your bag and go with him."

I might not have known what exactly was going on, but I did

know that the man who sat shaking before me was not the man I had married.

I didn't know what to do. How could we stay together? What kind of a role model would he be to my sons? Our children thought their daddy hung the moon. But I couldn't let them think their father's behavior was acceptable.

I had hoped he would snap out of it, recover, and return to his old self. But the man I married, the once energetic Tee, now slept most of the day, walked with a cane, and had stopped being a husband and a father. He had pushed aside the romance of our marriage and unplugged from the family.

I believed the church's teaching that divorce was wrong, and I never wanted my children to have to live in a broken home. I loved my husband, but if I didn't do something to stop what was happening, I knew I could lose everything—my family, my house, everything we had worked for.

I had to face the truth that I had been denying for three years now: my husband was addicted to prescription medication. I think the pain was just too much for him to handle. I never fully knew what combination of prescription painkillers or how many Tee was using. But I knew that at some point it became dangerous for Tee and for our family, and therefore it couldn't be tolerated.

Still, I felt conflicted. I had been with Tee my entire adult life. It's not an easy thing to walk away from your first love and the father of your children. When it came right down to it, though, I had to protect my family. We had been married for thirteen years, and I desperately wanted our marriage to work. I knew what it was like to lose a father, and I worked hard to make up for Tee's absence. But ultimately I knew his choices would be detrimental to our children. I could not allow it.

I did not want the kids to lose their father; I wanted them to have as much interaction with him as they could. But not when he was this way. Kids may be young, but they're not stupid. They see things. They start asking questions. And worst of all, they could get ahold of some of this stuff. What would I do then? Although I didn't know what would happen in our future, I knew nothing good would come for my children if I didn't stop it now.

So after hours of agonizing soul-searching and many tears, I decided that Tee needed to leave. I knew he wasn't going to leave on his own; even though he was unable to work or contribute to the family, I think he still felt a responsibility toward his children. And I believe he didn't really want to be the man he had become, but he was caught up in something bigger than he was. Deep down I hoped that my forcing him to leave would wake him up to the seriousness of the situation and that he would get help.

But I worried. *What's going to happen to us? How will this play out?* Even though I'd been raised in church, I still didn't know to say, "God, help me."

So I told Tee that his choice to continue misusing his prescriptions wasn't going to work, that the direction he was taking our marriage and family was not acceptable, and that he needed to leave our home. He nodded and said he understood. I think he had been expecting it. He seemed more relieved than anything. We were going to tell the children together, but he wanted to talk to them alone, so I agreed.

That night Tee sat with the kids and explained things to them. I could not hear what he was saying, but I imagined he was telling them that they needed to step up. Young LaDainian was almost nine, and knowing Tee, I figured he was telling him to assume the role of man of the house while he was gone.

My mind thought back to the day while I was pregnant with LaDainian that Tee asked me if I wanted a boy or a girl. As I watched small, serious LaDainian walk toward his bedroom, I knew that those little shoulders weren't prepared to handle such a large role of taking care of his mama. In my heart, though, I knew he would try because his daddy asked him to.

The kids went to bed that night without any tears, which surprised me. I assumed Tee's storytelling skills had brought them peace and direction. They might have been comforted, but I was scared to death. How was I going to support three kids? Who was going to watch them when I was at work? For a moment the fear made me reconsider, but when I thought again of those precious, innocent children, I knew I couldn't give in. So I watched Tee pack his bags and leave. I knew he would return to his Hill for comfort. And as my three babies slept, I stayed up all night wondering what would become of Londria, LaVar, LaDainian, and me.

I continued to hope that Tee would get his life together, but he didn't seem to be interested. I started to think that by kicking him out, I had actually given him more freedom, because now he could take his drugs whenever he wanted to without having to hide.

As the days passed, it became obvious to me that the kids hadn't completely understood Tee's explanation of the upcoming divorce. The months preceding my decision had been stormy, filled with arguments and tension. During those times, Tee had often left our house and gone to the Hill. He had often been gone for several days before returning. Now it appeared that Londria and the boys were waiting for their dad to come back as usual.

Every day one of the kids would ask, "When is Daddy coming home?" They didn't understand the change. Finally I had to sit them down and explain that Daddy wasn't coming home. That he was going to stay by Granny and their aunts and uncles and cousins. That he wasn't going to live with us anymore because his pain made it too hard for him to take care of his family. But, I reminded them, he still loved them very much.

That was such a difficult discussion with my children. Little LaDainian's eyes grew large as tears filled them. He nodded silently and hung his head. Tee was his hero. Now Tee was gone.

CHAPTER 7

Life on Our Own

I MISSED MARLIN. I was used to the open space of a small town. Waco made me feel claustrophobic. There were people everywhere. Even the air seemed different. After Tee moved out, we left our house, with its yard and fence and privacy, and moved into an apartment on the south side of the city. The apartment buildings around us were stacked and scattered like a child's building blocks. I signed a lease that I didn't fully understand, wondering if they could really make us stay for six months.

The first night in our new surroundings, I tucked the children into their beds and went back to the tiny living room. For the first time in years, I prayed. "Oh, God, what have I done? How am I going to support my family? How will I survive in this place?"

My soul longed for a piece of land and a real home. The children needed a yard with a fence where they could run and play safely. I stood and headed to bed, where I drifted off to sleep to the sounds of a couple fighting a few doors down, a baby crying, and a siren wailing. What had I dragged my children into?

The next day I looked out over the apartment building's courtyard and noticed all the children. I had never seen so many in one place—and all of them were left unattended. Some of them were just babies; I couldn't believe what I was seeing. *Where are their mothers?* I wondered. *Who's watching all these kids?*

This place certainly didn't have the same community feel that Marlin had. In fact, the simple things we had taken for granted back home were problems here. In Marlin, for instance, we could leave toys or bikes outside and nobody would touch them. But in this new neighborhood, anything left outside by our door was stolen.

Fortunately, Londria, LaDainian, and LaVar were unaware of the chaos. They seemed energized by the new faces. For so long they had played with their kin, their "cuzins." Now LaDainian would point to a strange face and beam as he told me, "Mama, that's my 'fend.'"

I was happy that they had "fends," but I'd never felt so alone in my life. I missed my family. My mom was ill, and my heart hurt that I was not there doing my part to care for her. I missed my sisters desperately. They were my best friends, and each was like a mother to my children. I longed for community. Back home, a host of people were ready to give me anything they had if I needed it. But in Waco, I learned to pray daily, "Lord, don't let me run out of something, because I don't know a soul I can borrow from." It wasn't so much a real prayer as it was my worrying about life in this new place.

When we had moved to Waco, I had to quit my job at HEB in Marlin and find one in this new place. Although I wasn't able to secure a transfer to the HEB in Waco, I was fortunate to find a job at a 7-Eleven convenience store not too far from our house. But on that salary, money was tight. We had what we absolutely needed but very little extra. I had my children to support, with no help from Tee since he wasn't working. I was also helping my brother and sisters support my mother financially.

I longed for someone to talk to, someone to lean on. But the people in Waco seemed too busy, too distracted, too overwhelmed. They had problems of their own and didn't want to take on mine. What had begun as a fresh start ended up bringing only fear, loneliness, and uncertainty.

Between the money situation and not feeling comfortable or safe having my children in this apartment complex, I decided if we were going to survive—financially and emotionally—in Waco, we were going to need to move. I knew I could be fined a penalty for breaking our lease, but I was willing.

It seemed that God had heard the cries of my heart and worked behind the scenes to take care of us. After five months, we left the apartment and moved into a house that was perfect. A newly built school stood right around the corner, so my children were able to walk there safely. And we had a fenced-in yard where the kids could play ball. I obtained a job at the HEB not too far from the house and applied for work at the Veterans Administration as well.

Then Tee came back into our lives. I missed him, the kids missed him, and he said he missed us too. So he moved in with us to try to reconcile. But Tee was still misusing his prescriptions. One day I came home from work and noticed he was acting extremely jittery. He kept pacing all over the place and couldn't calm down. I knew something was wrong. I had never seen him that bad before, and it scared me.

I tried to talk to him, but he wasn't able to focus. So I decided I would talk to him the next morning. But our discussion showed me he simply wasn't able to make the changes we needed for our family.

A few days later when I returned from work, he was gone. I knew he had gone back to the Hill. This time I knew it was for good.

|||

On our own again, I worried about paying the bills, as our lack of money continued to take its toll. I reached a breaking point one day not long after I had taken the kids shopping for school clothes. I had bought LaDainian two pairs of jeans that needed to last him through most of the school year.

After the first time I washed the jeans, I heard LaDainian call to me from his bedroom, "Mama, I can't fasten my pants."

"What do you mean you can't fasten your pants?" I called back. Dread filled my stomach. "Oh, God, please don't let those jeans be too small," I prayed as I walked into Dainian's room, where I found him struggling to button his jeans. They had shrunk.

How am I going to replace those jeans? I wondered frantically as I sat on the edge of Dainian's bed and cried.

After a moment, I realized my tears were not helping the situation. I composed myself and looked at my son. Fear and concern covered his face.

Immediately I realized I had broken one of my cardinal rules: never allow the children to worry about adult problems. They needed to enjoy their childhood, not shoulder my burdens. The worrying would be left to me.

I smiled at Dainian and gathered him in my arms.

"Oh, baby, everything's going to be all right," I reassured him. "We'll replace those jeans. Don't you worry about it."

Although I didn't know how, I knew I was going to make sure my children were always clothed and fed. That meant that some days I went without food so they could eat. I went without new clothes or items I wanted or needed so my babies didn't have to go without.

Londria, now a teenager, found work at the Boys Club of Waco, which later became the Boys and Girls Club. One day soon after she started her job, she came home and told me that we could enroll the boys there. I wasn't sure about this, because I thought the club was mostly for older children. But I agreed to give it a try.

The Boys Club far exceeded my expectations. They offered

tutoring to help with homework and organized activities such as swimming lessons. All three of my kids learned how to swim there. The manager and staff were wonderful with the children. My kids learned regulation basketball, including all the rules and correct terminology. And the coaches emphasized the importance of good sportsmanship. Little did I know what a huge part the Boys Club would play in Dainian's life.

One day, when he was nine years old, he came running into the house, sweating and out of breath. He held something behind his back, and by the look on his face, I could tell it was important.

"Mama," he began, "they have a football team, and I can play. It's for little people like me."

I chuckled. "For little people like you?"

"It's for boys my age, and they have a team for LaVar's age too. Can I do it, Mama? Please?"

"Well, let me see what it is," I said, reaching for the paper. It was from the Pop Warner youth football league.

LaDainian held his breath as I read the form for youth football. It turned out that he had done his homework—talked to the other boys, and knew in advance what was involved and how much it cost.

As I read the form, though, I noticed that in order to play, the boys were required to get a physical. We had insurance, but there was always the matter of the co-pay. Besides the physical, I knew there could be other hidden costs that go along with some of these programs. Money was already too tight. I wasn't sure I could justify paying for something that was not a necessity. But I was also concerned about the schedule. I was working different shifts at HEB and in food service at the Veterans Administration.

"We'll see," I told him.

His face fell. I thought about how much he had loved watching football with his father and how much he loved to run and play. I knew this opportunity to play meant the world to him.

This is the reason we moved to Waco, my inner voice reminded me.
So these kids could have opportunities they would not have in Marlin.

"Let me check it out," I said. "Okay?"

Dainian nodded.

I met the coaches and discussed the schedule, safety, and cost.
It would be tight for us financially, but I knew this was a dream
for Dainian. How could I tell him no?

I signed up both of the boys. LaDainian was so excited he
couldn't stop talking about it. He gave that program everything
he had. He practiced as long as he possibly could and even
begged to stay after practice to work on all the drills.

One day early on, one of the coaches told Dainian, "You
have to know where the football is at all times." Dainian took
that literally. Not long after that, as I tucked the boys into bed,
I noticed that Dainian was cuddled up with a football. I thought
it was sweet. Sleeping with his football.

But then the next morning he carried the ball into the kitchen
and sat down for breakfast, still holding the ball.

I must have looked at him quizzically, because he said simply,
"I have to protect it."

"Oh," I said and nodded.

From that point on, every time I saw Dainian, I saw that football. It didn't matter where we went, he kept that football tucked
under his arm. If he took a bath, that football sat on the edge of
the tub. If he watched television, the football was his companion.
I don't know what he did with it while he was in school. He was
a good kid, so I'm sure if the teachers told him to put it away
he did. But I can guarantee that wherever that ball was, Dainian
knew about it.

Of course, when you see someone carrying a ball like that,
what's the first thing you're tempted to do? Knock it out of his
arm! And that's what *everybody* tried to do—though no one ever
succeeded. His friends, LaVar's friends, and Londria's friends

constantly tried to nudge or push it away from Dainian. But he held on to that ball as if it were a military nuclear device!

The more he carried the football, the better he became at protecting it. And on the field, when he received the football, he never fumbled. It was as if that ball were an extension of him. Dainian had found his passion.

CHAPTER 8

Football for Little People

AT THE VERY FIRST Pop Warner practice, the coaches had assigned Dainian to the quarterback position. We were all excited, since that seemed like a great position—even though his football hero, Walter Payton of the Chicago Bears, was a starting running back. Every chance he got, Dainian practiced throwing the ball and calling plays. His role as a quarterback seemed to be a perfect fit—until their first game.

During one play LaDainian took the ball from the center and searched for an open receiver. There were none. So he tucked the ball against him, took off running, and scored a touchdown. The next thing we knew, the coaches found another quarterback and moved Dainian in as a running back.

He was thrilled! He was just like the man he idolized on the field. "Walter Payton is a running back too," he told me. "I'm gonna play football for the Chicago Bears, Mama."

"Not Dallas?" I teased. "I thought you loved the Cowboys."

"I do," he said seriously. "But Walter Payton plays for the *Bears*." He wanted to be just like Walter Payton.

|||

Because Dainian's life was filled with sports, the rest of the family's life became filled with sports as well. He went from one sport to the next: baseball, basketball, football.

When I wasn't working, my days were spent running kids back and forth for practices and games. And of course, the games weren't all in Waco. Some were in places like Austin and San Antonio, which meant we spent the entire day away from home. LaVar and the younger boys would play first, and then the older boys took the field. I would have to get Dainian and LaVar up early, drive them to the bus, and load them on. Then I would drive, watch the games, drive back, pick up the kids from the bus, and drive home. It could get tiring.

Fortunately, football parents are usually a tight-knit group and look after one another. That was one of the many perks of being involved with Pop Warner football. We were mothers to all the boys; they were all our sons. I often fed and kept many of the boys on the team until their parents could pick them up. I didn't mind; I was glad to be able to help.

|||

My sons were defiantly different individuals with distinct person-alities—and I loved them both fiercely. The boys shared a room, and their sides were as different as they were. LaDainian's half was as neat as a pin. His ribbons and awards hung in a straight row, his clothes and toys were neatly put away, and his bed was made to perfection. On the other hand, LaVar's side was so messy you could hardly get to LaDainian's half of the room.

It was the same with their chores. Dainian finished his; LaVar could barely *begin* his! I insisted that the children do their chores before they could go outside to play, and I soon discov-ered that LaDainian often helped LaVar clean so they could go out together.

But their differences were never more obvious than when they were playing football. As passionate as Dainian was about the game, LaVar didn't seem to share his enthusiasm. LaVar would just as soon watch cartoons or read a book or play with his toys as watch or play football. But Dainian could not get enough of it. If a game was on television, he was stationed in front of the TV. If anyone even mentioned football, Dainian perked up, ready to talk stats, players, and teams.

At practice, LaVar would sit on the ground, watch the cars go by, point up at passing airplanes, play with bugs and worms, and constantly ask the coach when it was time to go home. Always an active boy, he didn't understand why he had to pay attention and couldn't run around and do whatever he wanted. Although he enjoyed football, he simply wasn't all that interested in it. Dainian, on the other hand, begged to stay after practice to keep working on his skills. He didn't care if it was getting dark or he hadn't eaten all day. He would play through anything. Storms? No problem. Terrible heat? No problem. Broken bones? Really no problem!

His first broken bone was his arm. As much as Dainian loved football, I didn't want him playing injured. But at the doctor's office, Dainian talked to the doctor like he was daring him to say he couldn't play.

"Am I going to be able to play?" he asked.

"Well, what do you play?" the doctor said.

"I play little league." Dainian stared at that doctor with a look that said, *I dare you to say I can't play.* "Well, can I play? Huh? Can I play?"

Surprisingly, the doctor released him to play. "Well, if it's Pop Warner, I don't see a problem with you continuing to play," he told Dainian.

If I had been thinking fast enough, I would have said, "But he broke his bone *because* he was playing Pop Warner!"

Thank God for His protection, because Dainian simply didn't care about anything other than playing football. He stood in front of the coaches with his arm in a cast, telling them, "My doctor said I can play."

The coaches looked at me, eyebrows raised. I didn't know what to do. This was my first experience with sports injuries. Londria had never had a broken bone, but raising a boy was different.

Dainian looked at me. "Oh, Mom, please? *Puh-leease?!*"

"Are you sure, Dainian?" I asked, hoping he would somehow come to his senses.

"Well, yeah, Mom. Please, please, please?"

Well, I thought, *if the doctor said okay. . . .* I just shrugged, realizing I would have to tie that kid to a chair otherwise; there was no stopping him or slowing him down.

And before I knew it, Dainian was back in the game, attacking it with as much enthusiasm as ever. And I stood on the sidelines, shaking my head as I watched my son out on the field with a cast on his arm.

It was true love for Dainian. From then on, every time he'd suffer an injury, he would just keep playing through it until the game was finished. Only *then* would he let me take him to the doctor. When he broke his thumb, for instance, he wrapped it and then trotted right back out onto the field. I couldn't stop him; the kid was crazy.

After a while, I was almost afraid to take him to the doctor because I didn't know how Dainian would react if the doctor *did* tell him he couldn't play. I never would have heard the end of it!

There was only one time when he simply could not play, and that was in the sixth grade when he broke his foot. He was in a cast for what seemed to me to be an eternity. This kid was always going—if it wasn't football, it was basketball, baseball, running, playing outside, or riding his bike. Now he was confined to crutches, and I had to listen to the constant barrage of moans and groans and whines. I wasn't sure who was more excited for him to be rid of that cast—him or me!

|||

One day in the late spring, when LaDainian had played for several years, he brought home a form for Jay Novacek's football camp. LaDainian called it "the Emmitt Smith camp" because the Dallas Cowboys running back was going to be there. Emmitt Smith was one of LaDainian's favorite Cowboys.

Unlike the last time he'd brought home a form to play football, however, this time serious money was involved.

"Well," I started, "Mr. Jay Novacek isn't coming cheap, is he?"

But just like last time, I could tell by the look on LaDainian's face just how badly he wanted to attend.

"We'll see, but don't get your hopes up," I told him.

He knew that "we'll see" often meant no, and as I saw the disappointment wash over his face, I knew this time "we'll see" needed to mean yes. I had to do whatever I could to give him this experience.

Maybe I can work extra shifts to make the money, I thought. But would it be enough? It had to be. As I watched him walk from the room, shoulders slumped, I smiled. *He will be so surprised!*

I quietly took on extra shifts until I had the money for the camp. I filled out the form, and then I sat Dainian down and told him, "Dainian, you've been such a good son. You've worked hard and you listen well. I'm really proud of you. So I want you to enjoy going to that camp."

He was so excited I thought he was going to break down and cry right there! He could talk of nothing else for the days leading up to camp. Looking back, I am so thankful he was able to go, especially since while he was there, LaDainian had an experience that would change the course of his life forever.

While the running backs were practicing their drills, Emmitt Smith stepped into the line right next to my son and handed the ball off to him. At that moment, something clicked in Dainian's mind. He knew right then and there that he could and would make it to the NFL.

Dainian returned after that camp a different boy. He had always been focused, but now there was a fierce determination within him. From that point on, there was never a doubt in his mind that he was going to play in the NFL. It didn't matter that he came from a small town and didn't have the advantages others had. What mattered was that he now knew where he was headed, and he was determined to do whatever it took to get there.

CHAPTER 9

Rules for Protection

AS MUCH AS I LOVED and tried to provide for my children, there was one thing I could not be to them: a father. My children needed a man in the house—someone who could be a positive male role model to them on a daily basis. Of course they had great models in their coaches and teachers. But the boys, especially, needed a solid, steady presence in our home. Even though Tee and I were divorced and I still cared deeply about him, he simply was not in a position to turn his life around and be there for our children.

After our split, we attempted several times to reconcile. But Tee's focus was always on Tomlinson Hill. Tee felt he needed to be there to help his other children and grandchildren. One day I complained to him about how our children needed him as well. He shook his head.

"As long as you're alive, Londria, Dainian, and LaVar will be fine," he told me. "But there is so much that my other kids need. I have to be around for them. You can't fault a man for something like that."

So my kids and I made do the best we could. In the meantime, we continued to travel back and forth to Marlin for church services on Sundays and Wednesday nights. My kids and I enjoyed the connection with our family, and although we all hoped to see Tee during those times, we rarely did.

One Sunday about a year and a half after my divorce, we went to my sister Bertha's house after church for lunch. When we arrived, I was surprised to see a man there I had never seen before.

"Loreane," my sister said, "I want you to meet Herman Chappell. He's new to the area."

Herman and I connected immediately, and we talked the rest of the afternoon. He was originally from Oklahoma but had moved to Marlin to work in construction at the Veterans Administration. Like me, he had been married before and had children, so he understood what it was like to be a parent.

"I really enjoyed meeting you," he told me at the end of the day. "May I see you again?"

I was flattered and intrigued. Although I enjoyed his company, I was hesitant to get too involved with someone. I needed a man who could love my children and understand how important they were to me.

"I would love to see you again, Herman," I said, "but you know, I have three children and—"

"Bring them along!" he said.

"Really?"

"Absolutely," he reassured me. "I love kids."

I knew that a first date with all of us would prove whether or not he really meant what he said. I was relieved when I discovered he was telling the truth. The kids quickly took to him. And after that, they joined Herman and me on most of our dates.

At first Dainian held back a little; he was the man of the house, and he wanted to be sure about this man. But he was still so young, I think he was actually relieved when he saw that Herman was a good man. That meant Dainian could go back to being a kid without bearing the adult responsibilities that he felt he had to carry.

Herman and I dated almost a year and a half before we married. He was a good person and a wonderful family man. He could make me laugh more easily than anyone I knew. And he loved to spoil the kids. He made it a priority to do things with them and be involved in their lives.

Dainian was nine and had just started Pop Warner, and Herman joined me at every game he could. He built the kids a go-kart using a lawn mower motor. And when we talked about getting a trampoline to put in our backyard, Herman worked with the store assistant to set it up at 11 p.m. on Christmas Eve so the kids would have a great surprise for Christmas.

Most important, I could tell that Herman genuinely loved my children. And that made me love him even more.

|||

Even though the kids adjusted well to their new stepfather, they still missed their daddy. Unfortunately, the children's relationship with Tee was now mostly through telephone calls.

Though well meaning, Tee often made promises of gifts or visits that he rarely kept. The kids couldn't understand that the promises Tee made were dreams, things that he would *like* to do. He had health issues, financial limitations, and family obligations that prevented these things from happening. But no matter how many times my ex-husband slipped up, I made sure never to say anything negative about him. He was still their father, and he deserved that respect.

One day LaVar, still at a young, impressionable age, got off the phone with his father and ran into the room out of breath with excitement.

"LaDainian, did you know that Daddy's going to get us some ponies?" he asked.

"LaVar, what's the matter with you?" Dainian flared. "Don't you know that Daddy's not going to get us any ponies? He never does anything he says he's going to do! He lies to us!"

Something snapped in me as I watched LaVar's little face fall.

"LaDainian, don't you say that about your daddy! Who told you that about him?" I demanded as I pulled him into another room.

"No one told me," Dainian said. His frustration spilled over as tears filled his eyes. "No one told me! I've seen it happen, over and over. He says he'll come see us and he never does, or he tells me he's going to give me something and he doesn't! So now I know better. I know he's not going to do what he says!" Tears flowed down onto his cheeks.

"That's right; you learned that on your own. No one told you that your daddy wouldn't do what he says, so let LaVar find out the same way. He's young, LaDainian. There's no reason to burst his bubble. Let him make up his own mind about his dad, just as you did."

Dainian wiped at the tears with the palm of his hand. I knew he was hurt and felt terrible about his outburst. But I also knew that lashing out at his brother was really a reaction to the fact that he missed his dad and wanted so much to be part of his life.

The whole episode broke my heart. How I wished that Tee would follow through on his promises—that he would be the father Dainian, LaVar, and Londria really needed.

|||

Herman blended well into our family. The only drawback was that, like Tee, Herman was not a disciplinarian. If the kids asked him for permission to do something or go somewhere, he never told them a definitive yes or no. His answer was always the same: "Ask your mom."

I explained that as the children's stepfather he could act as their father. In fact, I encouraged him to do so! He always nodded in understanding, but then he would fall right back into the same role—good cop to my bad cop. I hated that I was forced to be the bad cop. But *somebody* had to do it.

I had been raised with a clear understanding of morals, of respect, of good etiquette. My daddy was a firm believer in corporal punishment, and he would deal it out as needed. While my mother very seldom spanked us, she often looked at us and said, "I will take you out! One more clean shirt will do you." It took years for me to understand that the clean shirt she referred to was the one we would need for our funeral! I'm not sure what I dreaded more—my daddy's punishments or my mom's cold stares and threats. They both managed to keep me on the straight and narrow.

Now as a parent to my children, it was my duty and responsibility to make sure they were raised with the same understanding of right and wrong. Not just because they needed to be well-balanced people, but also because I knew those things would keep them safe.

So I set clear-cut rules for them. Children need well-established boundaries to protect them and to let them know exactly what is expected of them. They thrive in that type of environment. My children were no exception. I laid the following ground rules:

- Show respect at all times to parents, elders, and especially teachers. I told the children, "Respect and honor your teachers. Never talk back to them. Treat them like you would me. You don't talk back to me; don't talk back to them."
- Speak politely to others. That meant the children were

expected to say, "Yes, ma'am," "No, sir," "thank you," "please," and "excuse me"—something Tee, Herman, and I instilled in them.

- Do not stay out past dark. I told them over and over, "I know you get caught up in playing. Time passes so quickly, and you want this time to go on and on, but it's your responsibility to be in this house. Not coming down the street. Not walking in the yard. *In this house.*"

- I didn't base their curfew on the streetlights, because sometimes the streetlight would be out. And then the kids would still be outside. They are so literal, you know. So I simply told them they needed to be in the house before that sun went down.

- Stay in the neighborhood.

- Follow the two-hour rule. Every two hours, the children had to check in with Herman or me, whether they were outside or at somebody's house. I also made sure they called me whenever they went somewhere new. If they were in the neighborhood playing at someone's house and they left to go to another house, I expected them to call and let me know where they were. It was important that I knew my children's whereabouts at all times.

- Treat girls with respect. Protect, help, and cherish them, even your sister. The boys were never to disrespect Londria. They were to help carry her things and open doors for her.

- No playing football in the house. This rule was difficult for LaDainian to keep sometimes. I came home once and discovered that a lamp in the living room had crashed to the floor and broken. LaDainian and his friend Steven had apparently decided to play in our living room. He got in big trouble for that one!

- No fighting. Although there was a three-year difference

between the boys and they were as different as they could be, they were very close and rarely argued or fought. Maybe they felt they needed to stick close to each other since their father was not around. Or maybe they just genuinely enjoyed each other. I only saw them fight one time. When LaDainian was twelve and LaVar was nine, I walked into a room and discovered them hitting one another. I was so shocked and heartbroken that I didn't know what to say or do.

"Stop, stop!" I cried as I pulled them apart. "What are you doing? How many times has your daddy told you never to hit each other?" I sat them down. "You two were put on this earth to love and protect each other. Friends will come and go, but the bond you have with a brother endures forever! If I should die—"

Their eyes widened and they burst into tears.

"Please don't die, Mama!" they wailed. "We love you! We won't fight. Please don't die!"

I lifted my hands and continued. "If I should die, you two will still have each other. You will share that history that no one else has. Cherish each other."

I never witnessed another blow between my boys.

I don't think my rules were unreasonable. I did my best to help the kids understand that those rules were for their own good, put in place because I truly loved them. I would rather have had my kids complain about my discipline than have to deal with a police officer's discipline or the world's discipline. My discipline always came with grace and love.

I believe Dainian understood that, because he always tried to be mindful of right and wrong. I never had a problem with that kid. He probably didn't like all the rules I had in our home, but he never disobeyed and he never mouthed off about them. I knew I could trust him to do what Herman and I expected of him. Because of that, I tried to find the proper balance and pick my battles wisely.

One night I heard screaming coming from LaDainian's room. I ran in to hear him yelling, "No, no, get the ball." I touched his forehead and found that he was burning up with fever. I rushed him to the emergency room, where he was diagnosed with severe tonsillitis. His temperature was at 103 and rising. The doctors gave him several prescriptions, and I brought him home.

The first night I held vigil by his bed—I'd never seen Dainian sleep the way he did during that time. He kept sleeping for two days and two nights, and his temperature continued to rise. My fears grew as LaDainian remained still and silent. But on the third day he woke up full of energy, and I felt he was well enough for me to return to work and let Londria watch him.

During my lunch hour, I swung by the house to check on the kids and found Dainian and his friend Don at the kitchen table. LaDainian was holding a needle and bending over Don, attempting to pierce his ear! I decided to let this scene play out because I didn't want to scare him and have him possibly injure Don.

"Don, are you okay, man? Am I hurting you?" a worried LaDainian asked.

"No, no, man, I'm okay," Don answered. "Just push the needle on through."

"It won't go through!" Dainian responded.

Don clenched his fist while Dainian pushed. Somehow LaDainian managed to pierce Don's ear. And as soon as he did, I made my presence known.

"What are you two doing?" I demanded.

The two startled boys jumped.

"Don and I made a pact," LaDainian began to explain. "We promised to pierce each other's ears. I just did his. Now it's my turn."

"Oh, no," I informed him. "No, no, no. I don't care about any pact you two made. You are *not* getting your ear pierced."

"Mom!" LaDainian argued. "I have to! We made a pact." Then he continued to insist on the great importance of their pact and how much it meant to him.

I finally relented. "Okay, okay. But you need to make sure you take care of it! I don't want you to get an infection or anything."

So Don pierced Dainian's ear. We inserted a small, thin straw into the hole, and every morning and evening I doctored his ear with alcohol. Then the boys purchased a pair of earrings and split them.

Although I was not thrilled about the piercing, I decided to allow it because in the realm of everything they *could* have been involved in—things that were much worse—this really was pretty low on the danger scale.

|||

Although I wanted to protect my children, at the same time I knew I needed to prepare them for the world. I often read the newspaper to the kids, focusing on stories about the trouble children got into. I wanted to illustrate the consequences of making wrong choices. I emphasized that they were to pay atten-tion to their surroundings and that if anything didn't feel right, if they felt tension in the air, they should leave immediately.

Herman and I had been married just a month or two when I received a call from my stepdaughter, Fi-Fi. Tee's son Charles had been killed. Charles was a wonderful, spirited boy, but he had always had a mischievous streak and was constantly trying to push the envelope. When Charles was twelve, for instance, I caught him smoking a cigarette. I was upset and told Tee, whose response was, "Boys will be boys. They like to try things."

I thought Tee had lost his mind.

"If you ever see one of *mine* smoking," I warned him, "let me know about it." I knew how he handled things, and I wanted to make sure the situation was taken care of right away.

I had always been concerned that Charles's choices might one day get him into trouble. And sure enough, one night he was in a bar and grill and began to talk to a woman. They started arguing, and she grabbed a knife and stabbed him to death. He was twenty-seven.

My kids were deeply affected by the brutality of Charles's death. The only other loss they had experienced was the death of their eighty-year-old grandmother. But she was older and they could understand that passing. Charles was so young when he died, and the manner in which he was killed was so shocking, that it really made an impression on them. Especially on Dainian.

Charles had played an important part in Dainian's life. Despite their eighteen-year age difference, Charles was always willing to spend time with Dainian. And whenever LaDainian would challenge Charles to a race—which was just about every time they were together—Charles always eagerly accepted, even though most times my son beat him.

Losing Charles changed us all. For me, seeing how quickly a young man can be snatched from this world filled me with fear. And I determined to watch my children even more closely.

"I know you can run fast," I told LaDainian, "but you still have to be watchful. Not everybody is your friend, baby. Not everybody will be good to you." It was so hard to tell him that, because I hated to take away some of his innocence, but I knew it was necessary.

About two years after Herman and I married, we moved into a beautiful white house with green trim on the corner of 27th Street. The backyard was fenced in, and we had several pecan trees on the property. The school was just down the street, and the neighborhood was quiet and peaceful and safe.

The kids could play anywhere between 27th Street and 25th Street. We knew several families, and we all watched out for the neighborhood kids. It was a good mixture of families, older people, and working couples.

One summer day when Dainian was twelve, however, we were all in the backyard when Tee's son Ron dropped by with some friends I didn't know. Herman offered them something to drink, and we all sat out in the yard chatting. The kids must have gotten bored with the adult conversation, so they went into the house. After a few minutes, one of the women got up and walked into the house.

I was shocked that she would enter my house without asking if it was okay, and as I sat there wondering about it, one of Ron's friends made a very offensive remark, catching my attention immediately.

"You need to leave now," I told him. "I do not abide that kind of talk at my house."

He scoffed. "I don't have to leave," he said.

Anger rose in me; I did not want these kinds of people around my family. I looked to Herman for some help, but he just sat there, suddenly taking an intense interest in his drink. I realized I was on my own. So I turned and faced this man square on.

"Oh, baby!" I said. "Don't tell me that you're not leaving. You're leaving! And right now. I will not need the cops to make you leave. You understand? The only reason we'll need the cops is for them to look down at your body and say, 'He's gone, ya'll. Call the ambulance.' They'll be carrying me off in handcuffs, but you *will* leave one way or another. This is *my* house. I pay the bills in this house, and you're leaving!"

Ron stood immediately and started to usher the man and

woman out, and just as he did, LaDainian came out of the house, eyes as big as saucers. He walked straight to me and whispered, "Mom, that woman in the house said some things to me that I'm not sure about."

"What did she say?" I asked.

"She said she wanted to kiss me and stuff like that," he whispered. He seemed embarrassed.

I exploded. That woman was Ron's age—thirty years old!

"I'll kill her," I stormed. "I'll snatch her bald and then I'll kill her." Just then the woman stepped back outside.

Ron seemed just as surprised and angry as I was. He ran to her and said, "Woman, are you crazy? That's my little brother!"

Ron pushed them toward the car, and as I watched them drive away, I realized things were not the way I wanted them to be. I had always led a sheltered life, and it never occurred to me that women would prey on young boys. The environment I fought so hard to maintain for the kids had become polluted.

CHAPTER 10

Finding Faith

ALTHOUGH I COULDN'T put my finger on it, something just wasn't right with our lives. I worked hard and tried to raise the kids right. But still everything seemed out of kilter.

Once a social drinker, Herman began to drink more frequently, and I was afraid it was escalating into a problem. He would often grab a bottle of alcohol and disappear for an evening, or even days at a time. I would tell the kids he had gone to visit his mother, and I would do my best not to allow them to see me worry or be upset about it, because I didn't want them to have to carry the burden of Herman's problems on their young shoulders.

One day after he'd been gone again I asked him, "How much do you drink?"

"I don't drink much."

"No, no," I said. "How *often* do you drink?"

"Oh, about every day."

"Every day?" I couldn't believe it. I guess I had been so busy, I hadn't realized how serious his drinking had become. I started to pay more attention then.

But it wasn't all Herman. I had taken on a few bad habits myself. I had been smoking cigarettes and drinking beer for a few years now, mostly to help me sleep. Even so, I knew I was drinking more than I should. I justified it by saying that I only smoked and drank when the children were not around. And it wasn't like I was doing it because I liked the taste; I simply liked the soothing effect they had on me.

Unfortunately, those soothing effects never lasted long. I tried not to think about what type of role model I was being for my children and instead fell into the "do as I say, not as I do" mentality. But the entire time I felt empty inside. My marriage was starting to wear thin and I was going nowhere. I was tired of always having to be the strong one—the strong parent, the strong spouse.

Although the kids and I still made our biweekly treks to Marlin for Wednesday night Bible study and Sunday morning services, somewhere along the line I seemed to have lost my way. Sometimes I wondered if the Lord even remembered me.

As a child, I had gone to church every Sunday. I went either with my father to the old country church his family had always gone to or with my mother to the neighborhood church with all our relatives and friends. In the church, I was introduced to the big, mean God who was ready to crush me into oblivion when I did something wrong and to the Jesus who was still hanging on the cross. But I didn't know the real, true, and living God. And church never really held a strong pull for me. It was more of a cultural activity than anything else. Going to church was simply something we did. But even at the age of five, I knew something was missing. I can still remember sitting in the church pew wondering, *Is this all there is? Isn't there more to it than this?*

Now, all these years later, my heart began to ask that same question again. There *had* to be something more to this life.

I had continued to attend church faithfully as an adult, but every Sunday we would go into the church and come out the same way—every Sunday, the same thing. I listened to everything the pastor said, but nothing really clicked. I was just going through the motions and "trying to do the right thing."

Somewhere along the way, I had lost what I really needed—God. Not a religious formality but a real relationship with God. I wanted that, especially as I looked at my life and realized that it wasn't working. My soul was hungry and longed to be fed.

One day I finally said, "God, I've made a mess of things. How do I get back to You?"

I got ahold of some Christian tapes and started to listen to them. As I did, I realized, *I am supposed to feel a peace with God. He's supposed to lead me throughout my life. He's a Redeemer. He is my true and loving God. I am made in His image; therefore, I am the righteousness of Him. If I reach out to Him, He will meet me where I am.*

"I believe that," I said aloud, "with every ounce of my being."

Around that time I began to mention my restless spirit to my sister Bertha.

"I've got to find a good church," I told her. "But I don't want the kind of churches where we came from. I want something that's real."

Bertha's mother-in-law was a pastor and had started a Bible study down in Marlin. So Bertha asked if I wanted to attend.

I had never heard of a woman pastor before, but I decided to try it, especially since Bertha spoke so highly of her and her teaching. And what a gift that woman had! She was a teaching, preaching machine.

She taught me how to read the Bible and ask God to show me His will. So I began to read my Bible diligently, and I began to experience such joy. He did not disappoint.

I also told Bertha that I wanted to quit smoking. She told me that the Lord helped her to quit smoking *and* drinking.

I was a little skeptical. "How does that work?" I asked. "Spell it out for me."

She told me that when you tell God you have a problem,

you just put it in His hands and trust Him with it. I was ready to break the habit, and I finally told myself, *This is the last pack of cigarettes that I will buy, and I'm quitting right now.* I had to make that declaration and believe it.

Then I put it in God's hands and trusted Him to help me. It wasn't easy, but I knew He was on my side and He would give me the strength to do it. I realized that even though God works with us, we still have to do our part. We have to do the best we can to fight our bad habits.

It seemed that the more time I spent discovering God's character and His love for me, the more peace and joy I had. Going to church was no longer a duty or an obligation but something I looked forward to every week. I was completely converted to Jesus. This is what I had been looking for, and I will always be grateful that God found me and my family.

It became important to me to teach righteousness to my children and to introduce them to Jesus. One day while I was having a conversation with God, I told Him, "God, You made me a loving and a conscientious person. I don't want to be constantly worried about my kids. You gave me a mother's instinct, and I can tell when something is wrong. I can't always be there, but You are."

And I heard Him tell me, *Trust Me with your kids. Watch your children and watch the people they surround themselves with. You will find that their friends are just like they are—good kids, with the same values.*

That day I gave my kids back to God, and I knew He was watching over me. I'd always suspected that He was, but now I knew. Also, I stopped smoking, drinking, and using words I shouldn't use, and I developed a great love in my heart for other people. The music in our house changed to gospel, and I began reading my Bible more. The kids were happy, and it seemed like our lives were coming together.

I started to watch, and God was right. They chose friends who were good, decent kids, and I thanked God for that. I looked at how they reacted in church, and I knew they really liked being there.

Even when they didn't know I was around, I watched as they bowed their heads and prayed. I listened to them thanking God, and I was pleased to see how their little hearts were so focused on our God. That was the part of my job I was most concerned about—instilling them with a sense of right and wrong and showing them Jesus. No longer was my motto, "Do as I say, not as I do." My life became, "Do as I do." I wanted them to see first-hand through my life the joy and power that come from following God and living a godly life.

||

God was clearly working in LaDainian's life too. When he was twelve, he had an experience that changed his life and faith forever, much more than football ever would.

One of his friends was going to a Christian youth camp for displaced and struggling kids, and he invited Dainian to join him. The camp was designed to provide a place for kids to get away from the stresses of difficult home environments. Since Dainian had a stable home life, he probably shouldn't have gone, but God wanted him on that trip for a reason. When he returned at the end of the week, I knew he was different.

I asked him what all he'd done and learned. He began to tell me all the funny, simple things kids learn at camp— things like cleaning your fork by licking both sides. But then he began to tell me about the other kids there, and as I listened to his stories, I realized how sheltered he had been. He had never had to worry about scavenging for his own meals, and he had a warm home to return to after camp. Some of the kids he met didn't know where they would be going once they returned home. Some didn't know where their parents were or even who they were.

While LaDainian talked about the mountain climbing and the other fun things he did, he talked mostly about the other kids and the struggles they faced in their lives. LaDainian did more soul-searching, more growing up, at that camp than he had ever done before. The experience made him realize that although his life on South 27th Street was good, life for other kids was anything but. Other children were going through things he had no idea about.

Over the next several weeks, Dainian began to ask me questions about our faith and why certain things happen to people and what our responsibility is in helping them.

"What do you do about something like that?" he would ask.

"Well, baby, we don't know where they're going, but we know that God knows. Everything that's going on in their lives, God will take care of because He doesn't lose any children."

I think that made him pray a little more for kids in general.

Several years later he stayed overnight with a friend who lived on the other side of town. Something happened while he was there, though to this day I don't know what it was. But when he came home, he was practically in tears and told me, "Mom, I'm so glad that you have always kept us in a safe environment and we stay in our neighborhood. It's safe and we don't have to worry about people coming by and grabbing us, and we don't have to worry about shooting and all this stuff."

I thought, *Where are you getting this from? The TV?* But then I thought, *You know what, this is not something I need to know.* God brought him out of it, and Dainian will never forget the experience. It's something that God did for him.

As I thought more about it, I began to wonder if maybe God had a message for me in the experience as well. Perhaps He was telling me, *I have plans for this child, but I'm letting you know he can deal with it.*

Dainian was good about coming and asking for my advice. Whenever he was having problems with something, I would say, "Well, let's pray about it. Let's see what God has to say." Dainian had a wonderfully strong faith even as a child, and it thrilled my heart to watch how he trusted and honored God.

As he grew older, he began to see that the passion he felt for football may have been placed there by God. Because I believed that God gives us dreams for a reason, I, too, thought it was possible that God was calling Dainian to a life of football.

But the closer I grew to God, the further from Herman I felt. I continually prayed for him and invited him to attend church with us. But even though he always made sure the car was clean and gassed up for our trip, he refused to go with us. He continued to drink, and I became more and more concerned that he might be addicted. Would his drinking lead to another situation like I had with Tee?

I wasn't sure, but I knew one thing. Whatever happened, God would take care of us.

CHAPTER 11

High School Life

TIME WAS PASSING so quickly. I couldn't believe LaDainian was already entering junior high school.

When he was twelve years old, his sister, Londria, got married and moved out. I wasn't crazy about how young Londria was to be getting married, but she was determined. The boys had always had to share a room, but now they were able to have their own bedrooms. Dainian was excited to get away from LaVar, since LaVar was so messy!

Unfortunately, Dainian's newfound "freedom" lasted only a couple of weeks. Herman's granddaughter Stephanie, who was the same age as Dainian, began to have problems at home, so we invited her to come live with us. That meant the boys had to room together again.

I felt terrible having to break the news to Dainian. But when I told him he had to move back in with LaVar, he never uttered a complaint. He simply said, "Okay." Then he gathered up all his stuff and moved back down the hall.

I might expect another child to say, "I just moved my stuff! Can't I stay a couple more days?" Not Dainian—he accepted his fate.

LaVar, on the other hand, was thrilled by the news! He said

to LaDainian, "You coming back? Good!" He knew that meant his room would be cleaned again!

Having just lost my daughter to marriage, I looked forward to having another girl in our home. I knew it was going to be a sad adjustment for Stephanie. I just prayed it would be a good adjustment. She settled into our family easily, and the boys really accepted her as a sister. She attended church and youth group activities with us. And she excelled both at home and at school. But I knew it was still difficult for her to be away from her parents. Sometimes at night I could hear her crying in her room.

I think one of the things that helped her get through the pain was her friendship with Dainian. They were in the same classes at school. And during football season she volunteered as the water girl or towel girl for the team.

What she brought to their friendship was her smarts—that girl was a brain. So she helped Dainian with all his studies. Although Dainian was good in school, he always had to work hard for his grades. My other children seemed just to glide through their studies with no problem. But not LaDainian.

Fortunately, in the same way that he focused on being a better football player, Dainian remained steadfast in his focus to do well in school. So when Stephanie came to live with us, he was excited that he would have a live-in tutor to help when he needed it. And Stephanie seemed to blossom from the sense of being needed and appreciated.

|||

Dainian's junior high years seemed to go by mostly without incident. He was running track and playing football, basketball, and baseball. One season ran into another, and his schedule was crammed with practices and games.

He was still committed to taking care of his body. And he

continued to use the weight set his dad and I had given him for Christmas when he was six years old. By middle school, he had a daily regimen to help him develop and build his muscles. He still worked long hours during and after practices on his drills, and he still carried his football with him everywhere he went!

It was around this time that he began to develop another habit that he would carry into the pros. One day during football season, LaVar came running into the kitchen, where I was fixing dinner.

"Mom, Dainian said that I can't talk to him!"

"What?" That didn't sit right with me because communication has always been important in our family. I put down the spatula and went off to ask Dainian why he thought he didn't need to talk to his little brother.

"Why can't LaVar talk to you?" I questioned.

"Because it's game day and I need to get focused."

Now, I don't know what he did all day at school—how he maintained this silence if a teacher called on him or if a friend wanted to have a conversation—but he was adamant about not talking . . . to *anybody*. Oddly enough, it didn't seem all that strange to me. Keep in mind, this was the kid who had slept with a football for years. So not talking on game day was just another of his self-disciplines.

I went back to LaVar and explained Dainian's need to focus and his request that we not talk to him.

"We need to honor and respect his choice," I told LaVar, and from that point on, we started leaving LaDainian alone on the days he played football. If our not talking with him kept him disciplined and focused on what he felt was important, then I was bound and determined to help him accomplish that. But I was certainly glad for the days when he *didn't* have games!

Poor LaVar—it was tougher on him, as he just didn't understand Dainian's need for quiet. LaVar liked to play football and sports—but to him, it was more of a hobby. By this time LaVar had started walking around with a notebook, writing poetry. He had varied interests, so it drove him crazy that Dainian was so obsessed with sports.

But LaDainian still held on to his dream of playing professional football. He believed it with all his being, and he stayed focused on that goal.

His obsession didn't bother me too much. It never affected his schoolwork—I wouldn't have tolerated that. He took his studies just as seriously as his football, although nobody could claim he had a passion for schoolwork!

He simply understood the importance of having discipline, even in the areas that weren't as fun or interesting. That discipline paid off in how he played. He was good—*really* good. Whatever ball he picked up—football, baseball, basketball—he seemed like a natural. I always sat in awe and amazement as I watched him on the field or court.

He was incredibly fun to watch! Because he had practiced and refined his skills, he could have more fun with the sports. In basketball, particularly, his sense of humor often emerged as he ran up and down the court.

He loved to play the clown. A player on the opposing team, for instance, might be dribbling the ball down the court, when all of a sudden Dainian would steal the ball from him. He would look around, eyes wide with fake surprise as if he'd won a prize, as if to say, *I got the ball?!*

He would then dribble the ball through his legs and do all sorts of other antics. He could do so many things with that basketball, I was sure that if he didn't make it into the NFL, he could always try the NBA. Or better yet, he could play for the Harlem Globetrotters! But there was nothing funny about how serious he was about playing and winning.

There was also nothing funny about the move our family was

going to have to make. My mother's health had been deterio-
rating to the point that the doctor informed her she was going
to have to have her leg amputated. My brother and sisters were
going to take turns helping her, but they needed me to be there
as well. After Herman and I discussed it, Herman offered to make
the thirty-mile drive between Waco and Marlin for work, so we
decided to uproot the kids and move back to Marlin.

|||

Going back to Marlin was a blow to the kids. LaDainian was
just entering high school, we had hit our stride in Waco, and
this move seemed like a step backward. However, I felt I had to
move back for my mother. My sisters and I took turns helping
her, and I tried—unsuccessfully—to make the kids happy.

I had hoped moving the boys closer to their father would
enable them to spend more time with him. But Tee continued to struggle with his addiction. I felt terrible every time
LaDainian and LaVar made plans for Tee to come see them
and then their father never appeared.

I learned that sometimes you just have to let sleeping dogs lie,
to use the cliché. They didn't talk about Tee too much, though.
By this point, I think they both understood what their dad was
dealing with. So whenever they said something or asked a question about their father, I simply answered, "Your dad will be okay
as long as you pray for him. God knows how to bring him out."

LaVar was much more willing to meet Tee where he was.
Dainian, on the other hand, wanted to help pull him out of
where he was and put him in a different place. Either way, I knew
the fact that Tee wasn't a part of their daily lives was frustrating
and painful for both of them.

Fortunately, some things were going well for LaDainian. He
entered as a freshman at Marlin High School and joined the

football team. During the preseason training, the coaches saw his talent and moved him up to the varsity team. During one of the practices, they matched him against the star linebacker in a one-on-one drill. The two of them stood alone. When a player handed LaDainian the ball, he not only ran at the older, bigger defender but ran through him. Everybody went crazy!

That year he played varsity football, basketball, and baseball. The basketball coach was very fond of Dainian. His wife told me on several occasions that the coach thought as much of LaDainian as he did his own son. I felt so honored by that remark.

But as great as all the coaches in Marlin were, Dainian and the rest of us were miserable. We had leased out our house in Waco for one year. Fortunately, my mother wasn't as bad as we thought. She got a prosthesis and learned to walk on it. After I talked with my sisters about our situation, they agreed that our mother would move in with my sister Bertha and she would take care of her.

So after one year in Marlin, we moved back to Waco. The most difficult part of the move was telling the coaches. Not surprisingly, they all encouraged us to stay. They recognized LaDainian's talent and knew he would make a big contribution to their teams.

"You can't take him back!" they complained. "Please stay here! Rethink your decision." It was difficult to feel like we were letting them down, especially Coach Greene, but Waco was calling us back.

We moved back to Waco in time for LaDainian to start tenth grade and to play varsity football for the University High School Trojans under Coach Leroy Coleman.

Even though LaDainian played on the varsity team in tenth grade, he was not the starting running back. Coach Coleman believed that each player should earn his spot on the roster. Since an older boy was an upperclassman and got to play that position, Dainian played fullback and outside linebacker. While he eyed the coveted running back position, he still got plenty of playing time, and it seemed that every time I turned around, his name was in the paper.

I didn't necessarily agree with the choice not to allow LaDainian to play running back, but I never interfered with a coach's decision. I often saw other parents telling the coach what they thought needed to be done. It seemed that they all had an opinion about where or when their child needed to play.

But I believed it was the coach's right to mold a player, and his decision needed to be respected. I always told LaDainian, "You never know when a skill you learn, such as training for a position that you don't like, might pay off in the end. How many times, for instance, have you seen a quarterback throw a block to keep the other team from scoring after an interception? It happens."

Still, there were times when Dainian would be standing on the sidelines looking sad, and of course that made me unhappy too. So after a game or practice, I tried to make it a point to talk to my son and listen to his concerns and frustrations. LaDainian and I grew so close during these talks. He knew that I was always in his corner. But he also knew that my advice was going to be the same: stay the course and listen to your coach. Your time will come.

No matter how much he disliked the position he was playing, he knew that quitting wasn't an option. Throughout his whole life, he had always heard me say that there are no quitters in this family. He always kept his eye on his dream. And even though it was difficult for him to watch someone else in the position he felt he was born to play, he continued playing to the best of his ability.

I believe ultimately that's what made him a true leader and champion. Being a leader and showing respect is a big part of team sports. After all, as I often told LaDainian, "You can only control your own actions. So you need to make sure that you're doing what *you* need to do."

That came back to haunt him several times—mostly *off* the field.

One of my pet peeves had always been cars that drove by with their music blasting. I thought disturbing people with loud music was disrespectful.

"Don't ever do that, got it?" I would say to Dainian if a car happened to drive by with its stereo thumping.

"Yes, Mama," he always replied.

You can imagine my irritation when one afternoon he returned home from football practice in his friend's car with the music blaring so loudly that my windows were shaking. I ran out of the house in time to see Dainian stepping out of the backseat of the car.

"*Why* is that music so loud?" I asked. "How many times have I told you about that? You know we have elderly neighbors, and I won't have you disrespecting and disturbing them and others."

I'm sure I embarrassed LaDainian by carrying on in front of his friends, but I felt strongly about how disrespectful he and his friends had been.

"What am I supposed to do, Mom?" he asked. "That's not my car, and I'm not the one driving."

"I'll tell you what you are supposed to do," I continued. "You ask them to turn down the music. And if they won't, you get out of the car before you enter this neighborhood, and you walk the rest of the way! When you leave this house, your actions represent our family, and I will *not* have you showing disrespect."

To some, this may seem like a small thing. But to me, it was important that LaDainian understand that his actions represented our entire family.

I know peer pressure was one of the biggest problems my children faced, but if Dainian truly wanted to be a champion, he needed to understand that includes being a leader, not a follower. And showing concern and respect for others on a daily basis is a wonderful quality in a leader.

|||

Warm breezes swept over University High School, and love was in the air. LaDainian had just attended the junior-senior prom with his girlfriend of two years. His junior year was winding down, and all seemed right with the world. The family liked his sweetheart, and she fit in easily with the crowd of friends that was always present in our home.

Keisha often confided things to me that Dainian never would. As close as he and I were, I knew there were some things that he just couldn't tell his mama. And Keisha let me know if he had a need or a problem that he was reluctant to share with me, so I could help him.

One afternoon, for instance, she told me that Dainian wasn't drinking enough water during his workouts. He wanted to keep his weight at a certain number, and he had chosen a very danger-ous way to do it.

After I read him the riot act, she looked at him and said, "See, I told you I was going to tell your mom."

His romance wasn't the only thing that was blooming in LaDainian's life. He was excelling in all of his sports. Although he was still playing fullback, there was a light at the end of the tunnel. Senior year was beckoning, and he hoped that his time would come to play running back.

While Dainian's plan to play in the NFL had been formulated when he was nine years old, he knew there were steps he had to take before pro ball was even an option. His heart and attention were on the one thing he had worked so hard for over the past three years: the starting running back position. Coach Coleman had worked with him and molded him, and now Dainian had the chance to show the world just how much potential he had.

But unforeseen events threatened this plan. Things on the home front were not going as well as they were on the playing field. Herman's contract at his job had ended, and I hated my job. Herman had searched high and low for employment, but at the time, jobs that fit Herman's skills were scarce. He was competing with students from Baylor and others who seemed more adept to the changing job market. He was finally able to find work in Garland, a suburb of Dallas—115 miles from Waco.

So while LaDainian was eagerly anticipating his senior year at University High School, I had the unpleasant task of telling him that it wasn't going to happen; we were moving to Garland.

CHAPTER 12

The Letter

AS BEAUTIFUL AS SPRING in Texas is, dark clouds can move in and, in a red-hot minute, produce a storm so strong that it can rip off the heads of our beloved bluebonnets. Looking at LaDainian's happy face, I would have sooner faced a Texas tornado than tell him we were moving, but I couldn't put off telling him the news.

"Dainian, baby," I began, "I have something I need to tell you." I calmly explained the multiple reasons our family needed to relocate and how sorry I was that we were going to uproot him from school and his friends.

He jumped from his seat.

"Mom, *no*! Please, no! You can't take me away now. The scouts won't know where to find me!"

"What are you talking about?"

"Mom, this is my senior year."

Oh yeah, I realized. *He's been waiting to be the starter.*

Now, I guess maybe I had been thinking that the football scouts and Santa Claus had something in common: they both could recognize the good boys and know where to locate them, no matter where they moved. While Santa brings toys, a scout can give the gift of education and the opportunity to be seen by the recruiters of the NFL.

I tried to explain that Garland had an excellent school district with a fine football program. It broke my heart to see my son so distressed. I realized that Dainian was a special case. Playing professional football had been his dream. And with one move I could destroy it. He had worked so long and hard for the starting position, as I'm sure the young man had in the Garland school where Dainian would transfer. Dainian wouldn't be able to waltz in and take over the spot that someone else had earned. Sitting on the bench his senior year in Garland wasn't an option—even I knew that. On the other hand, we didn't have a choice. He needed to come with us.

LaDainian thought otherwise and came up with many creative options.

"What if I stayed with a friend?" he begged. "Hey, I know one of the coaches would keep me!"

"Dainian, you don't understand," I told him. "That's too much to ask someone. You are too young to be on your own. Whether you think so or not, you need your parents and we need you. I'm sorry, but you're coming with us."

Dainian must have done some praying, because God started to deal with me. God began to whisper into my soul, *Look at your son. He's responsible and he does what he is told. You've trained him to know the right path to be on. He'll be all right.*

I thought back to a time early in Dainian's high school career. He had asked to go to a party in east Waco where I didn't know the parents or the surroundings. I was against the idea, but he pleaded with me. Finally I agreed. My child hadn't been gone thirty minutes when he returned. The ride over to the party and back took that much time, so I didn't understand why he was home. When I questioned him, he told me that he didn't feel right being at the party. As it turned out, he'd made the right choice. Shortly after he left, a fight broke out.

Dainian was a responsible boy, and he made good decisions.

I knew his sixth sense had developed and he could judge a situation on his own. He had matured and was ready to make more decisions.

So I considered my options, opened my mind, and listened to God. I had seen families in this situation before. When they needed to move, their kids would stay behind. When I thought about all the coaches who had worked so hard with him, I began to rethink the whole thing. I would be taking their starter. I realized my final decision would affect more than just me and my family. Finally, the peace of God came over me and allowed me to know that everything I had instilled in LaDainian was still there.

While God was working on my heart, LaDainian was working on other people's hearts. He must have told everyone in the world that his mama was making him move! We began getting telephone calls from coaches and teachers, friends and teammates. Even Londria and her husband discussed it, but they were busy with their baby, my precious granddaughter, Nikki.

One day, a few weeks before we were set to leave, I found Rose and Emmitt Hughes standing on my front porch. They were good friends of ours and neighbors who lived two blocks over on 25th Street. Their son, Jason, was a year younger than Dainian and in the football program.

I invited them in. They barely got settled onto my couch when they cut to the chase.

"Did you know we recently added on another bedroom and bathroom to our house?" Rose asked.

"I heard something about that," I said.

"Well, you definitely need to come by and see it."

"I would like to do that," I responded. I had suspicions that there was something more to this impromptu visit than a discussion of their new home addition.

"We'd like LaDainian and Stephanie to stay behind, live with us, and finish their senior year at University High."

I was stunned. "We can't do that!" I insisted. "That's too much to ask of anybody."

Rose and Emmitt were the finest people on the earth. They had similar values to mine and were strong Christians. I knew if I were to choose anyone to care for my son, it would be them. They used a similar structured discipline, and they always knew where their children were.

I knew Jason and Dainian were close friends, but how would this work? Would we pay rent to Rose and Emmitt?

When I started to ask questions, they explained that they didn't want a dime to keep the kids. They were even willing to offer Stephanie the new addition. They understood that since both LaDainian and Stephanie were seniors, it wouldn't be fair to allow one to stay and force the other to move. Jason and LaDainian could stay in one room together. They had twin beds, and they thought the boys would get along fine.

While I appreciated their generosity, I still wasn't sure how it would work. I thought about what we would need to do if we did accept their offer. I would need to always make sure that Stephanie and Dainian had their lunch money and everything they needed. LaDainian had his car and a bank card, so he could get their supplies and take them where they needed to go. If additional expenses came up, like schoolbooks, he could use the bank card to get the money and take care of it. He was such a responsible young man, I knew I could trust him.

This is crazy! I thought. *I can't leave my child!*

Then my mind went back to Dainian's face when I told him that we were leaving, and I looked into the eyes of these people who were offering to shelter and care for Stephanie and my son for a year. God and I had made an agreement a long time before: He would watch out for my children when I couldn't be there. I felt that He had put this loving couple in our lives for a reason. He had worked everything out. So with appreciation and deep pain in my heart, Herman and I accepted their offer. LaDainian and Stephanie would stay in Waco at University High School, while LaVar went with us to Garland. I would trust the Lord to hold them in His arms.

When LaDainian arrived home later, I said, "Have you been talking to Rose and Emmitt?"

"Well, I did tell them that you were going to move us to Dallas," he said.

"You know they came by."

"What did they say?" he asked. He seemed afraid to ask, yet afraid not to.

"I guess you're going to stay here with them. Emmitt and Rose have offered for you guys to stay."

"Really?!" He was so relieved and excited.

Just then Stephanie came into the room.

"Well, Stephanie," I said, "do you want to go with us or stay here?"

She looked shocked for a second before she completely recovered. "I want to stay here!"

"Stephanie, you get the better end of the deal," I continued, "because that room addition they just put on is yours."

Stephanie screamed, and LaDainian kept saying, "Thank you, Mama!" I thought they were going to pass out from the excitement!

It was still a couple of weeks before we left, and those were the most difficult days for me. Even though I knew that God had arranged it, it was still hard to leave my kids. Rose was a good friend of mine, and I knew the type of parents she and Emmitt were—no-nonsense churchgoers who ran a tight-ship household like I did. But still I struggled through the separation.

I never dreamed I would pack my bags and move to another city without LaDainian. But too soon we packed and left Stephanie and my little "cookie monster" behind.

|||

The dog days of Texas are grueling. In August temperatures hit triple digits and stay there for weeks. When you take a deep breath, it feels like it sears the lining of your lungs. While most of the population is sitting in front of air conditioners, though, a special breed of young men is layering on extra padding, saddling up, and heading out for their workout during the hottest part of the day. For them, it's just another football practice.

Football is a religion in the Lone Star State, and in small towns, where high school football is a way of life, our teams and their members are revered. Our coaches are trained to cope with the heat and protect their players as best they can. But we all know that the boys are taking a pounding and sweltering for hours during those drills.

Then just when you think you can't take another minute of the heat, a cool breeze will sneak in from the north, and you get an excited feeling in the pit of your stomach because you know the time is here. It's Friday night and time to go to "church": the local stadium.

Now, Mama may have moved to Garland, but when her baby was playing football, she burned up the highway to get where she needed to be in time for the kickoff. The anticipation began before we even left the house, and my body was always flooded with a thousand emotions.

Arriving at the games, we stood in line and bought our tickets like everyone else. Yet there was the knowledge that I was somehow different. I was offering my son, my baby, to a sport that is so brutal it had injured or even nearly killed some of the players who had gone before him.

My eyes always scanned the crowd for other football moms, my support group. While some people came for an evening of entertainment, we football moms came to witness our children being attacked and knocked down over and over again.

Seated on the bleachers, I watched the drum corps beat a steady cadence as the cheerleaders danced and moved to the rhythm. The beat grew stronger and stronger as the anticipation grew. The hair on the back of my neck began to rise, and the skin on my arms felt a tingle as goose bumps began to appear.

I watched as the warriors burst through an outstretched banner and rushed onto the field. My eyes always searched for LaDainian. I was somehow comforted when I saw the familiar number 5 leading the pack. He seemed changed, transformed, from the boy I knew so well. His facial features carried the focus of a man well beyond his years. The laughing, friendly son who begged for more cookies was gone, and in its place I saw the beginning of what I somehow knew was going to be a legend.

As each game progressed, if a player went down, my heart stopped until the player was identified. And even if the fallen player wasn't LaDainian, the fear remained, because I was a mother to every boy on that team. Worried eyes connected with other football moms, and the prayer was always the same: *God help us. Let him get up and be fully restored.*

Then the relief flooded our bodies as the player rose and assured the trainer that he was okay. But there were times when the player didn't get up and was taken off the field. This limbo— the period of time when we didn't know the extent of the player's injury—was maddening. I felt as though I couldn't breathe, and yet I kept an eye on the game because my son was still fighting the battle.

Then in the midst of all the concern, LaDainian would break loose, turn on the speed, and score a touchdown—six points on the board. To my son, it was a token to God, a small part of fulfilling a destiny that seemed to have been waiting for him since before he was born.

During every game, I experienced the same thing: a rush of emotion flooded me as the crowds rose to their feet and cheered. I felt as if I had been on the field, and I ached from the high levels of adrenaline that were pulsing through me—the fear of the injuries, the thrill of the touchdowns. And then the battle was over. If our team scored a victory, I felt a small compensation for the punishment my son's body had taken. However, if the points fell short, I knew that he would carry a pain in his heart that was far worse than the physical ache.

Every Friday night was the same experience.

We were pleasantly surprised to see how many games LaDainian played in the Dallas area. Those games were more convenient—some just around the corner. It really didn't matter where they were playing, however, because I was there. Nothing was going to keep me from that!

|||

One thing I had noticed from middle school on was that each year the boys got bigger and bigger. But quite frankly, Dainian wasn't growing at the same pace. So by senior year, when Dainian took the field, it reminded me of the biblical story of David and Goliath. The first time I saw my little "David" face the new and improved "Goliaths," I felt concerned. Each one of those giants had one desire: to stop my son any way they could.

But on the season opener of his senior year, my son ran, spun, and dodged the giants just fine. He was well trained and knew what he was doing. Of course he took hits, but he stayed focused and kept his mind on the game and not on the pain. And even though Dainian was smaller than most of the other players, he set a rushing record for his high school.

With pride we watched him work his magic, and soon we found ourselves involved in the state championship. A perfect way to end a fantastic season would be to capture one of Texas's most cherished prizes: the title of state champs. But after making the drive to San Antonio, we were shocked to see the Calallen team from Corpus Christi. Each one of their boys was bigger than two of ours put together. After a hard-fought battle, we lost.

I knew this was going to be a disappointment to Dainian. But when I found my son in the crowd, I was surprised to see him smiling and surrounded by a mass of people clambering for his autograph. Girls were shouting his name and offering different things for him to sign. They had everything you can imagine: big footballs, little footballs, programs. Adults were pushing their children into the pack to get an autograph.

There he stood, tired but happy, patiently signing as many autographs as time would allow. I turned to Dainian's girlfriend and said, "This is the beginning." I don't know how I knew it then, but I had no doubt in my mind that this was just a small sample of things to come.

The sting and disappointment of losing the state championship gradually faded, and when all the dust settled, LaDainian had amassed several honors during his senior year in football. The 2,554 yards gained and the thirty-nine touchdowns he'd made that year brought him the District 25 4A most valuable player award, the Super Centex Offensive Player of the Year honor, and a spot on the second all-state team.

It was not long before letters of interest from colleges started coming in. I stayed out of the picture when the subject of college came up. LaDainian had hopes of attending a college that was highly recruited by the NFL, like the bigger schools in Texas or Oklahoma. How could I offer advice to someone who could pick a letter from a pile and recite from memory everything about that school's team? He knew what each school's win-loss record was, the formations they used, and which player held the running back position. He knew what division they were in, their stats, and most important, how long it would take for him to get a starting running back position.

Even though I wasn't helping him make his decision, he still kept me informed of his whereabouts once college recruiters began flying him to colleges all over the United States.

On Saturday mornings he would call and say, "Guess where I am, Mom?"

Then he would tell me that they had flown him to see a certain school and their facilities. Somehow it never occurred to me that he was flying in winter and there were bad conditions in a lot of these states. The thought that he might encounter weather so bad that it would stop a flight plan dead in its tracks never entered my mind.

So after LaDainian had traveled to a wide variety of states, it came as a shock to me when I received a call from a coach saying that Dainian was stuck in Denton, Texas, of all places. The weather was so bad that they had grounded his plane.

The coach told me not to worry, that he was going to stay with Dainian until the weather cleared. I told him I was grateful and said if it looked like it was going to be too long, I would drive from Garland and sit with him. But his flight finally got off, and when he called to tell me he was home, I said, "Thank God!"

In the meantime, LaDainian moved on to basketball and track. His basketball career seemed to be going really strong as well. Coach Lloyd's training and work with Dainian brought scouts to those games too. One in particular was from Baylor University, although I didn't know who he was at the time. I was trying to watch the game while this man kept trying to talk to me. Baylor ended up offering him a four-year scholarship to play basketball. Even though he was honored and the Waco location would have been convenient, his answer was no. His passion was football.

· |||

While LaDainian had big dreams, he was like any other teen-ager and faced his fair share of temptations. One day in the early part of his senior year, I had a dream that Tee, one of Tee's brothers, and Dainian had been drinking together. I sat straight up in bed. I knew Tee wasn't drinking with my son because I had told him I would kill him if that ever happened, but I also knew from the intensity of the dream that it was a message from God.

First thing the next morning, I called the school and asked to speak to my son. They told me they couldn't get him out of class.

"Listen," I said. "I am in Garland. My son goes to school there. I *need* to speak with him. It's very important."

"I'm sorry," the administrative assistant said. "I can't pull him out of class."

"Well, put me through to Coach Coleman."

As soon as the coach got on the phone, I said, "Coach Coleman, I need to talk to Dainian. It's important."

"I'll get him," he said immediately.

Dainian's familiar voice soon sounded over the phone.

I didn't even waste time asking how he was.

"You've been drinking!" I told him. It wasn't a question; I didn't want to know. I just wanted him to know that I knew.

He didn't bother to deny it; he just broke down and sobbed into the phone.

"Dainian."

"Ma'am?" he said, sniffing.

"Okay, now that I know this, we have to decide what we're going to do about it. Why did you even try to drink? Didn't you know I would find out about this?"

"No, ma'am," he replied, still sobbing.

"Well," I said, "you know that God shows me everything. Alcohol will take you down and you won't be able to do the things that you've vowed to do. So this is your first and your last time. I mean that. I will not let you throw your life away."

"Yes, ma'am."

I wanted him to realize how serious this problem was. He was going to have to decide what he was going to do, because I was ready to haul him up to Garland with us. It might not have been the best career choice, but I didn't care; I had to save my son. I trusted him, and I believed that conversation was going to take care of what he was doing.

A few days later I grabbed the mail and noticed a letter in LaDainian's handwriting. We still saw each other almost every week, so I couldn't understand why he would need to write me a letter. I ripped open the envelope and pulled out a single sheet of notebook paper.

I read his handwritten words:

Hello Mom, how are you doing, I guess your wandering why I am writing you a letter when I can talk to on the phone or face to face. The reason is I want this letter kept until I forfeel my goals, and when I am feeling low I want to look at this let-ter and remember what I said on this letter. Mom I love you so much that every time I say it or write it, it brings tears to my eyes. One day you will be the proudest Mom in the whole world, because I'm going to go to college and graduate and if God is willing go on to play pro football. And be the best person I can because that's how you raised me. Mom I thank you so much for everything you have and is still doing for me, becaus it is hard not having a father who I could talk to and get advice from. You did the very best.

(Sorry so sloppy. Kept crying.)

Love, LaDainian

Oh, I cried. I knew his letter was sincere, and I knew it was like a plea: *Don't stop believing in me.*

The next time I saw LaDainian, I threw my arms around him and gave him a tight hug. "Dainian, I love you so much!" I told him. "And I believe in you. I have always believed in you. That will never change. Through your life, you will be faced with choices, and you may not always make the best choices. But you have to remember that there are consequences for making those choices. And I don't want you to fall in the cracks and get lost."

I knew my son. When he told me he wouldn't drink anymore, I had no doubt that he was telling me the truth. And thankfully the issue of alcohol didn't raise its ugly head again until the end of his senior year.

A group of Dainian's friends had picked him up from his girl-friend's house and driven a few blocks when a police car pulled them over. The officer said that he had smelled marijuana as they drove by. No one in the car had any, but an open, empty bottle of alcohol rolled out from under the driver's seat.

At the time, Dainian was seventeen and the others had turned eighteen. So he was escorted to the Hugheses' home, and the officer had a talk with Rose. That evening the family gathered and LaDainian told them he had no idea there was anything like that in the car. He explained that the boys had just picked him up and were giving him a ride home.

Rose made the dreaded call to me. After hearing that no charges had been filed against him, I was calm. I knew that once I had busted Dainian on something, it would never happen again. He had earned my trust during the last episode, and I believed what he said when he claimed to have no knowledge of the open bottle in his friend's car.

Later we learned that the mother of one of the boys had encouraged her son to tell the police that the alcohol was LaDainian's because he was still a juvenile and they would go easier on him.

LaDainian was hurt and disappointed that his "friend" would lie like that, but it taught him to be careful about whom he hung around with. He quickly learned that being in the wrong place at the wrong time with people who are practicing dangerous behaviors can take you down just as fast as if you were doing it yourself. People are often judged by the company they keep.

|||

Now LaDainian's goals seemed to hit a roadblock. After many trips to different schools and a fair amount of recruitment, the message came back loud and clear: "Size matters!" The recruiters didn't think he was big enough to compete with the giants who had continued to grow. It didn't seem to matter how well he played; they still saw him as a second-tier player.

Also, many of them suggested that if LaDainian had played running back his junior year and compiled the statistics that he did in his senior year, he would have drawn much more attention from the bigger schools. As I understand it, a player's junior year is very important to recruiters. That information is considered and some selections are penciled in based on those stats.

So not playing running back until his senior year may have figured into the lack of big school offers. Even though his senior year stats were stellar, only three schools offered him a full scholarship: University of North Texas in Denton, Baylor in Waco, and Texas Christian University in Fort Worth.

He narrowed it down to two—the University of North Texas and Texas Christian University. UNT practiced on artificial turf and TCU didn't. Since not all schools had artificial turf, he didn't want to spend a lot of time practicing on it because it is harder on the body. And he thought being close to home would make it easier and more affordable for us to attend the games.

When he told me he was leaning toward TCU, the only thing

I said was, "Oh, really? Okay, so TCU it is!" I wanted to make sure this was his decision, that he never felt pressured based on what he perceived to be my wishes.

So on National Signing Day in 1996, Herman and I drove down to University High School in Waco and watched LaDainian sign a letter of intent to the Horned Frogs of TCU. He was one of only two players who received a full college scholarship. I thanked the Lord for providing, because I had no idea how we were going to be able to afford sending Dainian to college without a scholarship.

National Signing Day was an *event*. Herman and I were at Dainian's side as he signed his letter. Photographers and reporters were everywhere. So were radio stations, television reporters, and newspaper journalists. It was a really big deal, and I had never experienced anything like it before.

Every weekend during the football season, LaDainian had been the guy to watch, so this was big for the local media as well. Every now and then, a kid would come out of high school with a full four-year scholarship. In Dallas it happened more often, but not so much for Waco. So that made Dainian's signing even bigger.

As I stood there glowing with pride over my son's accomplishments, I remembered the letter he had written that was still in my purse. My son had just taken the next step to fulfill his promise in the letter: to go to college.

PART THREE
TEXAS CHRISTIAN UNIVERSITY

You'd never guess from this adorable photo that I had the most colicky child ever born. This photo managed to capture one of the few moments in LaDainian's babyhood when he wasn't screaming!

Finding the money for LaDainian (left) and LaVar to participate in this Pop Warner youth league team meant a lot of extra shifts at my two jobs, but it was worth it to have the boys spending time together and building memories.

Teaching my children to walk closely with Jesus was my number-one goal as a mom. When we went to church, we always invited our friends, relatives, and neighbors to tag along—it made it more fun for us all. Here are the boys ready to go (LaVar on the left, cousin Stephen in the middle, LaDainian on the right).

This picture reminds me of one of my most precious Christmas memories. I had to work all of Christmas Day at the VA hospital, but I rushed home at lunch for some time with my family. I couldn't believe it when Herman and the kids surprised me with a "mother's ring," decorated with the birthstones of all of my kids.

Baseball, basketball, football—LaDainian went from one sport to the next. My days were packed with work, my evenings with driving to various practices, and the weekends with games all over Texas! Sometimes Herman and I would have to split driving duties, and we'd pass each other on the road, each of our cars packed with kids in the backseat.

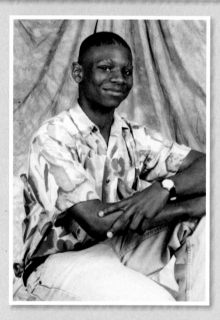

Sometimes you just have to let your kids be kids. I have no idea why LaDainian decided to shave his eyebrows for his school portrait— but when you consider everything a teenage boy could possibly get up to, I guess strange-looking eyebrows aren't so bad.

My wonderful firstborn daughter, Londria, probably saved me from going crazy in a house that seemed full of boys!

Hello mom, how are you doing, I guess your wandering why I am writing you a letter when I can talk to on the phone or face to face. The reason is I want this letter kept until I ~~feel~~ forfeel my goals, and when I am feeling low I want to look at this letter and remember what I said on this letter. Mom I love you so much that every time I say it or write it, it bring tears to my eyes. One day you will be the proudest mom in the whole world, because Im going to go to college and graduate and if god is willing go on to play Pro football, And be the best person I can because thats how you raised me. Mom I thanke you so much for every thing you have and is still doing for me, becaus it is hard not having a father who I could talk to and get advice from. You did the very best.

(sorry so sloppy kept crying)

Love, LADAINIAN

This letter from LaDainian is one of my most prized possessions. To this day, I carry it with me wherever I go.

One of the many jobs I held throughout the years was nursing assistant at the VA hospital. While it was rewarding in many ways, I saw so much suffering on that job that it broke my heart; I knew it wasn't the career for me. However, it did give me utmost respect for health care professionals, like Stephanie (Herman's granddaughter), who became an RN.

Once LaDainian decided to attend Texas Christian University, his remaining days of high school sports sped by in an exciting blur. Before I knew it, I was sitting next to him on National Signing Day as he made a commitment that would shape the next four years of his life.

LaDainian wore the number 5 in high school, and it was such an important part of his identity that he asked prospective colleges if his lucky jersey number was available. He was disappointed that he couldn't carry it through to the NFL because running backs have to wear numbers in the double digits.

There wasn't much time to hang out with LaDainian after his college away games, when they're loading up equipment in trucks and busing the players back to the airport, but we managed to sneak in a quick hello after this game in Nevada.

It was such a thrill to be with my son when he received the prestigious Doak Walker Award, honoring the country's best college running back. I go back for the ceremony every year to represent LaDainian (I've only missed once!), and it's always a great time.

"If you're not prepared to lose, then don't play." That's what I told my kids when they were growing up, because I wanted them to be able to handle life's inevitable defeats graciously and with class. I was surprised that LaDainian didn't win the Heisman Trophy, but when I saw him congratulate the winner with a big smile, I couldn't have been any prouder of him if he had. We're pictured here with TCU coach Dennis Franchione and his wife, Kim, along with the elusive trophy.

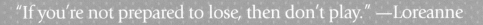

"If you're not prepared to lose, then don't play." —Loreanne

This photo was taken in Marlin the last night Tee was with the kids before he died. They ran into each other in town and spontaneously decided to have dinner together—something that usually happened only once a year or so. There is no doubt in my mind that God arranged that special night so the kids could have the memory of one last dinner with their dad. (Pictured, left to right: Tee, cousin Rodney, LaDanian, and friends)

This photo of "the boys"—Carl (my sister Mary's son), Brodreck, whom we all call "André" (the son of my late sister, Bertha), LaDanian, and LaVar—was taken at LaDanian's condo during the first year he played for the Chargers. There's a special bond between these four first cousins. They have fun together and watch out for one another, and here they are taking advantage of a few rare moments of guy time on the balcony.

I'm usually the one taking the family photos, so I'm often not in them. But when this picture was snapped, there were plenty of people around to do the job! It's from our first-ever family reunion. In a small town like Marlin, everybody is pretty much considered family. We probably had at least 75 people coming and going that year, and the number keeps growing.

LaDainian's wife, Torsha, impressed me with her intelligence, friendly spirit, and beautiful smile from the first time we met. She has made my son so happy, and I can't imagine the family without her.

I love this photo because it reflects something I've often heard LaDainian say to me: "I have a job doing what I love to do!" He really takes joy in the sport, the teamwork, and the opportunity to help others . . . and it shows.

On November 19, 2006, LaDainian became the fastest player ever to score 100 touchdowns—89 games with 102 TDs! Here he is scoring the "big 100."

LaDainian celebrates his first touchdown of the December 17, 2006, game against the Chiefs. At that moment, he surpassed the most points in a season by an NFL player—a record that had stood for 46 years. If there was ever a time to do a celebratory dance, this would have been it, but actually I think the camera just caught him mid-move. I've never seen him celebrate a touchdown since his Pop Warner days; he prefers to simply hand off the ball and keep going.

"I have a job doing what I love to do!" —LT

Walter Payton was LaDainian's childhood hero. (Today he even has a dog named Sweetness, after Payton's nickname.) Just imagine his sensation when he passed his hero on the all-time rushing touchdown list with his 111th career rushing TD during this game.

Since 2002 LaDainian has celebrated Thanksgiving by meeting with underprivileged families and handing out turkeys.

LaDainian is a man of few words. I know he was honored to receive four ESPYs in 2007, but he doesn't talk about his awards much. When we talk, it's mostly about family or the kids he helps through his humanitarian work. Trophies and sports memorabilia will be fun to show your grandkids, but what's more important— and more lasting—is how well you loved your fellow man.

CHAPTER 13

TCU, Here We Come!

TEXAS CHRISTIAN UNIVERSITY is located in Fort Worth, Texas, "where the West begins." The northern boundaries of the city boast a genuine stockyard that still parades a herd of longhorn steers up and down the brick pavement daily. Some of the local watering holes have been there since cowboys settled their disagreements with shoot-outs in the middle of the street.

As you leave the stockyards and head south, you will come into a downtown that is so electric you can feel money being made. Skyscrapers hold the movers and shakers who dabble in everything from oil to advanced technology. And before you get the impression that this is some hick town, drive through the museum district and have a taste of the art displays that rival those in New York City. If you are looking for something a little more colorful, try the Cowgirl Museum and get a taste of what our female pioneers endured.

Speaking of color, if you head a little farther south down a street called University, you will find the campus of Texas Christian University, where everyone's blood takes on the school's color: purple.

TCU is nestled in the shade of hundred-year-old oak trees, and the manicured lawns are green and lush. If you are expecting cacti and tumbleweeds, forget it; the historic buildings are columned, and some are vine covered. The bells tolling from the steeple in the church remind you that this is a Christian university. This was where the football team, the fighting Horned Frogs, lived, and so would my son LaDainian, who had signed on to become one of them.

LaDainian had already moved into his dorm during the summer since he had to be on campus early for football training. I had wanted to drive him over, but he said he was okay to go on his own. That was the first twinge of pain I felt in letting my boy go. A distant cousin of ours was on the coaching staff at TCU, and I took comfort in that because he promised to be there for my son.

Within a few weeks, though, I couldn't stand it anymore and called to tell Dainian I wanted to visit. He found some free time between all the drills and practices, so Herman, LaVar, and I made plans to drive from Garland to Fort Worth.

On the way, I said a prayer that Dainian would cling to and grow in his faith as a believer in Jesus. My small-town insecurities surfaced, and I worried about him being happy there and making friends. He is shy by nature, but once you get to know him, he is likable and easy to get along with. As my anxiety rose, I recalled God's promises that my children would be okay. And I knew LaDainian had chosen this school to be close to his family, so I pushed my doubts into the recesses of my heart and put on a brave face.

We drove onto the campus, and I was impressed by its beauty. I walked around the campus, LaDainian's new home for the next four years, and thought, *Loreane, we sure aren't in Waco anymore.*

|||

I had known since National Signing Day that this time was coming. I'd experienced this once before when my daughter got married and moved out. Now it was LaDainian's turn. As we gathered around the table at University High School in Waco, I realized what the stroke of the pen in LaDainian's hand meant. He was going to live in Fort Worth and play football for Texas Christian University.

I wouldn't be in the next room calling to him that dinner was on the table. There would be no scanning his face to judge his mood. Sometimes I could tell more about his day from looking at him than by what he said. Now we would be connected by a phone line and I would have to have faith that if he had a need he would tell me.

Yes, we had been separated during his senior year of high school, but I felt like I had just gotten him back. Now he was off to college, where I would lose him again—but this time for good. He was transforming into a man, and he would no longer call my home his home. He was off to make his own path in the world.

I wondered, *Will I ever have my son back?* I knew I could still mother him over the holidays or special weekends here and there. But it sure didn't seem to be enough time. At least I had a little time left with LaVar before he moved on! That definitely helped me deal with emptying my nest.

We pulled into a parking space by his dorm and got out. He was there to greet us with a huge smile, and I knew right then that he would be really happy here. He was surrounded by football guys, so they had common ground. He was doing what he loved. It was as though he was saying, *This is the next phase of my life, and it's going to be good.*

I wanted to be able to feel that same way. But watching my son already settled into his dorm room at TCU left me with a strange mix of emotions. He was filled with excitement and anticipation of the future. This was a major step toward fulfilling his dreams. And I had never been more proud of him.

But I have to admit, when I looked at him, my mind saw

a man but my heart still saw a little boy. My baby who stub-
bornly carried his baby bottle around, who fell and scraped
his knees, who cried when his daddy left. My sensitive and shy
little boy with a gentle spirit who loved to run to his mama
and hug her. A gentle spirit is not the norm in football, and I
wondered if this new world would crush him. Would his sensi-
tivity be able to withstand what the world was going to throw
at him?

For a moment I wanted to scoop him up in my arms and run
back home with him. But I knew this was the moment I had prepared him for his whole life—the moment when he would leave
my protection and home and become a man—his own man. My
head knew it—but my mother's heart ached.

Leaving Dainian at this school where he didn't know a soul
was one of the most difficult things I had ever done. Worry
clouded my mind. What about the hazing that goes on in colleges—would that be a factor here? I'd never heard about anything like that at TCU, but who knew? And I wasn't sure how
anyone got an education with all the distractions and parties.
LaDainian had promised me that he wouldn't get involved with
any "silliness." We both knew that even one misstep could ruin
his dreams.

All of his life, I had been there to balance the brutality of
football with a strong maternal love. The separation we endured
during his senior year in high school was bearable because of the
strong support group I'd left him with. That year had obviously
been a good thing for LaDainian because he became indepen-
dent. This move didn't seem to faze him.

But now I had to turn my back and walk away from this place,
leaving him with nothing familiar except the number 5 that he
would wear on his football jersey. In a strange sort of way, it
brought me comfort to know he was able to carry this number,
the one from his high school football days, to TCU.

We hugged, and he smiled that big, beautiful smile of his.

"Thanks, Mama," he said. "I'll be okay. I love you."

"I love you too, baby."

I tried to hold back my tears until we were in the car.

Oh, God, I prayed as we made the drive back home to Garland. *Keep him strong in You. Keep him strong in his body. Give him health. Keep him safe from those college seniors all over the country who are the size of houses waiting to knock my baby down. You're all he's got. Hold him close, Lord.*

My emotions were in such turmoil. If I had thought rationally about it—which was difficult at that point—I would have realized that I was really the one who was afraid, not LaDainian. He was thrilled! But somebody had to worry for and about him! There were big boys there who were going to try to beat up on my kid out on that field.

Okay, pull yourself together, I told myself sternly.

I looked out the car window at the traffic racing down the road beside us. Like a warm blanket, God's comfort began to wrap around me as He reminded me that I had promised to leave my children in His care when I couldn't be there. I knew I didn't have any choice. Even though I felt that I was throwing Dainian into the deep end of the ocean and walking away, I knew it was the right thing to do. When a mother holds on too tightly, she can cripple or kill what she is desperately trying to protect. I didn't want to do that to my child. I knew I had to let him go.

My role now was to assure LaDainian that he was ready for this new life and to step back. So by the end of that day my mind and heart were in agreement—he was a man. And I knew two things: this man had a big job to do, and TCU wasn't running a "Mommy and Me" football program, so I needed to go on.

|||

LaDainian was fine . . . better than fine. With God as his protector and a five-man front line whose combined weight was rumored to be more than 1,500 pounds, LaDainian Tomlinson was able to work his magic and break one record after another.

Around that time, LaDainian began to wear the visor that he would eventually become famous for. He began having migraines and issues with his eyes, so a local doctor recommended that he start wearing the visor. (It helped and, of course, he continued to wear that visor throughout his career.)

As his freshman year progressed, many of my worries began to fade. He quickly fell into a routine of classes and football practice, and he and his roommate began what would become a lifelong friendship. He also found a church to be involved in.

There's a big distinction between being a child in a godly home and being an adult making your own decisions about God. I wanted his faith to be his own—something he found strong and powerful in his life.

The first time I visited, I asked how he was doing with God. He sounded genuinely happy. "Good, Mom," he told me.

"What do you like about the church you've found?" I asked.

"The pastor is good," he said. "He has really good messages that make me think, and they have a good choir. I enjoy going."

Those words filled my heart with joy.

When I left LaDainian's room that day, I wondered how he was going to make it without me. But the answer came swiftly. He was doing so well that it kind of hurt my feelings. I wanted him to need me at least *a little*! I would try to help him and he would let me know that he didn't need me. If I offered to drive over and make him a meal or do his laundry or take him shopping, he'd refuse.

"No, no, Mama," he'd say. "I'm okay. I've got it under control."

These young men are a new breed; they can take care of themselves.

Even though Herman, LaVar, and I saw LaDainian every weekend for games, I still looked for excuses to call him during the week. He had his own vehicle, so I often called to ask him if he needed gas money. I did this to give him the opportunity to say, "Oh, Mom, it's so scary over here." But he never did say that. As a matter of fact, he would be the last person in the world to say that. He could be thrown into any situation, and he always seemed to find his way.

Whenever we visited him in his dorm room, he would ask us if we wanted something to eat. We'd look around the tiny room and ask where he was going to get food. He'd disappear down the hall, then return a few moments later with his arms filled with chips, dips, and soft drinks from the snack machines.

We sat in that cramped space and talked and laughed and had a ball. Those times always reassured me that he was happy and healthy.

That was off the field. On the field was serious business. Pat Sullivan was LaDainian's head coach. In 1994 Coach Sullivan had led TCU to a 7–5 record that was good enough to win the Southwest Conference (SWC) title. That hadn't happened since 1959, so we felt like the team was under good leadership.

We knew that because Dainian was a freshman, he would not be the starting running back. Basil Mitchell was the starter. But still Dainian went in chomping right at his heels.

It seemed like all the pieces were in place for a victorious season. LaDainian had been so successful his senior year in high school that we felt he would make a positive contribution to TCU. We knew that these college teams were composed of some of the best talent in the United States and that the competition would be tough and exciting. Every time I thought about it, I would get butterflies in my stomach. This was the big time, and we were ready to rumble.

Even my role as a mother was different now. For starters, when I arrived at the ticket booth, I showed my ID and was presented with complimentary tickets—and they were good seats. When my son was in high school, I'd shelled out ticket money just like everyone else. So this unexpected perk was very welcome, especially considering all the money I had spent on travel and football expenses over the years!

Also, some of the rituals and traditions that had been part of our experience since the Pop Warner days just didn't work at the college level. For instance, I had always followed the team bus to the games. Since the youth league days, Herman and I had always made sure we got there early so we could form a caravan with other parents and fans.

Of course we could have gotten there faster if we went on our own. But that bus carried our beloved sons who were pursuing their dreams. Following them was a show of support, and I had every intention of keeping that tradition alive while Dainian was in college. When our guys played home games, the stadium was on campus, so there was no need to follow them; they were already there. And most of the away games were so far that we either didn't have the time to go or couldn't afford a trip that would involve overnight accommodations.

It wasn't until they played an away game in El Paso that I realized I would never be able to follow the team bus again.

My husband, my sister Theopal, and I had driven to the game in El Paso and were returning home when I caught sight of the bus. The police were stopping traffic to let it on the freeway. I got choked up emotionally when I saw cars pull over so a vehicle that contained my son could pass. *Things are different now, Loreane,* I realized. Football players at this level were given special respect and privileges.

As we saw the bus headed onto the freeway, I asked Herman to get behind the bus so we could follow them home.

My sister chuckled and said, "What are you talking about? We can't follow the bus home. They're flying!"

"What do you mean they're flying? They are in a bus!" I argued.

"Yes, they are in a bus that takes them to the airport," she said with a laugh.

"What airport? What plane?" I felt so confused.

All this time I'd thought that LaDainian was taking a bus to the away games, even the ones that were out of state. When we got home, I called LaDainian with a thousand questions. I asked about the planes, what they looked like, how big they were, how safe they were, and anything else I could think of.

It seems funny to me now, but back then it threw me for a loop. My son had been flying all over the place and never thought to mention it to me. And to this day I have never seen my son get on a plane, even in the pros. I always watch him load on the bus and drive off.

When I first discovered that some of LaDainian's away games were so far that I couldn't go to them, I wasn't too worried. I was foolish enough to think that all the TCU games would be televised, so I could simply watch the ones that weren't local. When I realized they weren't on TV, I panicked.

Turning to the radio, I moved the dial up and down looking for his game. When I hit a station that had someone calling out the action, I was elated until it dawned on me that what I was listening to had nothing to do with TCU. So I turned the dial again in hopes of finding the right game.

Sometimes when I found it, the signal was so weak that it had static or faded in and out. This wasn't something I wanted to experience when I knew huge men were trying to stop my son.

And whenever I heard an announcer say that my son was down, I sent up the prayer that had been born in youth league: *God, let him get up. Get up, Dainian, get up.*

Not being able to attend every game was one of the hardest adjustments I had to make. But it turned out that during LaDainian's freshman year we had very little to celebrate. With Coach Pat Sullivan at the helm, we were filled with optimism and ready to start the season. The smile was quickly wiped off our faces, however, as our team lost its first game. We muttered all the old phrases like, "We'll get them next time," and we still held high hopes for a great season.

After losing the next few games, we told ourselves that sometimes it takes a while for a team to gel. Sure, there was still time for a good season. But as the losses continued, we began to walk out of the stadium with our heads down and shoulders drooped.

After ten straight losses, the jury was in and the verdict was devastating. Never in our lives had we experienced losses like this, and this was the big time. We weren't driving around the corner for a Pop Warner game. Some of the parents, fans, and alumni had flown in from all over the country to see our boys play. It was heartbreaking.

After the tenth loss, I told Herman, "You know, I don't think Dainian is going to be able to take this." I worked my way over to the tunnel to catch him. And sure enough, as soon as he caught my eye, he broke down into tears. I knew he needed an emotional release, and I was glad I was there to comfort him.

"Hang in there, LaDainian, better things are yet to come," I said. "Remember, all of these colleges have recruited the best players available. The boys who couldn't play are still at home. So the competition is stiff. You have excellent players on your team. They just need something to pull them together. It's going to get better."

As I was comforting my son, the assistant coach, who was a distant relative, came over and said, "Come on now. This doesn't look good. Come on with me, LaDainian. He'll be all right."

That just cut right through me! I felt that it was my duty as a parent to comfort my devastated son. Yes, there were people gathered around watching—and most of them were as upset as we were.

"No," I told our cousin. "He is crying because he *feels* this game. He puts everything he has into it. If he didn't care he wouldn't be so upset. You ought to be glad that he cares so much! These kids came here to win. They didn't come here to lose. You all need to pull this thing together!"

I felt like that season was a breaking point for those boys. Every last one of them was extremely talented. They all had "the right stuff" and were capable of winning. At the time I couldn't figure out what was missing from the picture, but I knew something had to change. God had brought us too far to let us fail like this.

|||

The summer after the losing season, while he was at training camp, I got a call from Dainian. "We got a new coach," he said.

"Oh, LaDainian, that's wonderful! There will be new programs, and things are going to turn around!"

But the other end of the line went silent. Suddenly I sensed that I was the only one on the phone who was excited.

"Dainian?"

"I don't know," he said finally. "I don't think I'm going to like him."

Surprised to hear this, I asked him why he felt that way.

"Because he's got me playing fullback, and I don't like playing fullback," he replied.

Well, I thought my prayer had been answered. I wanted someone to come and pull things together. Perhaps the new head coach, Dennis Franchione, was just what we needed. Although Dainian wasn't happy about playing fullback, I knew that everything would work out. Anyway, we had nowhere else to go but up.

CHAPTER 14

A New Coach

WAVES OF CHANGE swept through the TCU football program. Dennis Franchione, "Coach Fran," started with the basics. The call went out: "Everyone to the weight room." Football players in a weight room are nothing new, but the intensity of the program, once reserved for a select few, was. Our Horned Frogs were giving up the flab, and hard bodies were emerging. Along with the workout came a high-carb diet that seemed to fuel their bodies and desire for victory.

LaDainian attacked the weight room with a new vengeance. Weight lifting had been a passion of his since he received that beginner set at age six. But under the direction of Coach Fran, he was able to improve to the point that in his junior year he would go on to win TCU's Iron Man award. By then he weighed 210 pounds and was able to bench-press 450 pounds.

During his sophomore year, though, he used those workouts to release some of the frustration he felt. His dream of being the starting running back was put on ice when the coach moved him to fullback. He hated it. He felt like he had a lot to contribute to the team, and this position limited him. And although the coach gave him a lot of playing time, Dainian was still unhappy.

When he initially told me that he was unhappy about playing

fullback, I wasn't too concerned because LaDainian always worked through problems pretty quickly. He wasn't the type to linger on one thing; he just moved on.

I knew that the starting running back, Basil Mitchell, was a senior, and Dainian was next in line. If he could just hold out until next year.

I told him, "It'll be okay. Just work through it. Help the team."

And he was all for that, but he wanted me to know that this wasn't easy. I could sense that there was something different about this situation. It was another setback.

Over the years, LaDainian had always struggled against one unforeseen circumstance after another. People told him he was too little to play football. And when he broke his foot and couldn't play for a while, a bigger boy took his place on the team.

Although he had healed enough to start football in middle school, he was still not 100 percent, and by the time he had healed enough to join the high school team, our move to Marlin derailed him again. When we moved back to Waco for his sophomore year, he was already behind those who had played as freshmen. Had he been there all four years he might have been given a shot at the running back position his junior year, which would have possibly given him a shot at one of the bigger schools.

LaDainian respected and understood each of the decisions the coaches had made along the way, especially when he was in high school. Those coaches worked hard to help their seniors get noticed by the scouts. But now that he was in college and his next goal was the NFL, he didn't feel that his football career could take another setback.

LaDainian's best chance of getting into the pros was to play running back as soon as possible in college and let the NFL see what he had. So after the third game, LaDainian knew he couldn't handle playing fullback any longer. He even started to question whether or not he had chosen the right school to attend.

Lance Williams, one of Dainian's good friends, told him, "Man, don't worry about playing fullback—you're going to get your play. Someday your name is going to be up in lights and there will be billboards with your picture. Just hang in there."

Although Lance's prophetic remark did encourage LaDainian, I still sensed a discontentment in him that made me worry. There had been so many changes in my son's life in such a short time that I suspected it was catching up to him.

He had a passion and a drive that couldn't be denied, and he'd had too many setbacks in the past not to recognize another one when he saw it. So he knew what he had to do, and he placed everything on the line.

All through the years LaDainian had followed his coaches' orders and played whatever position they wanted him to. He had tried to follow Coach Fran's plan and had played several games as fullback. But finally he knew he needed to have a man-to-man talk with Coach Fran. He explained calmly that he was better suited for the running back position. And in a courageous, heartfelt moment he told his coach that he was seriously unhappy. He knew what was in him: the ability to be a great running back.

When I found out LaDainian had confronted the coach, I knew he must be truly miserable. He doesn't like conflict, so for him to gather his courage and face this mountain was an important step in growing his character.

He knew that if Coach Fran would give him the opportunity to do what he did best, he wouldn't be sorry. LaDainian promised to give him everything he had. Running the stairs at the stadium in the heat of the day when others had long since gone home. Working out late into the night when others were studying or sleeping or hanging out with their friends. LaDainian would do whatever it took to achieve his goals, even if it meant working harder than anyone else.

After Coach Fran listened carefully to LaDainian, he said, "Okay, you're right. I'll change you."

|||

LaDainian made all kinds of changes his sophomore year. But one change that knocked me over started with a simple phone call: "I'm moving off campus." It seems there was a room shortage, and he and Greg were leaving the dorm for an apartment.

Now mind you, I was just starting to accept the fact that he was safe in the dorm, so his moving into an apartment with no supervision left me in a panic. There were too many distractions waiting to pull him off course. And it wasn't long before one of those distractions, a friend I'll call Bob, came along and parked himself on LaDainian's sofa.

You've heard about someone who comes to dinner and stays forever. Well, Bob and LaDainian had been friends in high school.

During LaDainian's sophomore year of college, good old Bob began attending the games and spending the night at the apartment. Then, it seems, it became easier just to stay with the guys during the week and save the drive time up to the games. The problem was, Bob wasn't working or going to school. Personally, I think he was watching TV, playing video games, and mooching.

This wouldn't have been such a problem if Greg and LaDainian had endless supplies. But they weren't allowed to work because of their scholarships. So Greg's parents and Herman and I helped with the things that the scholarships did not cover, like gas, food, and other incidentals. We were all under the impression that the boys were doing fine until LaVar went for a visit.

LaVar reported back to me that Bob was extending his stay indefinitely and the guys were running short on provisions. He told me that all they had to eat was noodles.

I called Dainian and asked him, "How you all doing on food?" I had never had to ask him that before.

"Oh, we're okay," he said.

"Well, what are you all eating?"

"Noodles."

"LaDainian, how long have you been eating noodles?"

"Um . . ." He hesitated. "Several days."

"You mean you don't have milk or anything?"

"We're all right."

I couldn't believe it. "Why didn't you tell me that you were running short on food?"

"Well," he said, "I know that you don't have a lot, and I didn't want to bother you."

"LaDainian, helping you is not a bother! You need milk and good nutrition to be able to be healthy and play your best!"

So I ran out to the store and purchased bags of groceries and took them to the boys. When I arrived at the apartment and knocked on the door, Bob answered. He seemed glad to see that I was bringing more provisions!

When I got a chance, I took LaDainian aside.

"Bob needs to go," I told him. "If he were going to school, I could see it. If he were working, I could even see you and Greg helping. But Dainian, you all can't afford this. You guys have never, ever been like this."

"Yeah, I know," he said.

"What does he do all day?"

"Nothing," Dainian admitted.

"Does it not upset you that you and Greg both get up and leave and go to class all day and then to football, and when you come home all tired, he's just sitting there? That doesn't bother you?"

Dainian nodded and finally told Bob he would have to leave.

LaDainian was very busy on campus with football and his studies. He had entered school pursuing a degree in TV/radio announcing. But somewhere during this time he changed his major to psychology. Maybe it was because of his experience with Bob!

Nevertheless, I'm sure there were times he missed the carefree days of high school, when there was more time to hang out with his friends. One of the hardest lessons Dainian learned that year was that an old friend can be a major distraction to achieving your goals.

LaDainian was a caring, trusting man. And college is a time when many young people blow off steam and have a good time. But my son knew that he was on a path that had a very small margin for error and he needed to remain focused.

Of course, that didn't mean he didn't do anything crazy. LaDainian didn't drink, smoke, use profanity, or get into trouble. He did have one vice, though. LaDainian loved tattoos. During his freshman year in college, he got several tattoos on his arms: hands folded in prayer; the number 5; and his initials, LT. I was not thrilled when I saw them, but I admit I was touched by the tattoo he got his sophomore year.

One day while he was visiting our family at home, he unveiled his left shoulder. There I saw a tattoo of my likeness. And under it were the words *My Inspiration*. It told the world about his love and devotion for me. It was special. Unfortunately, whoever tattooed him misspelled *inspiration*. It read *inspiretion*.

Londria laughed.

"Hush, girl," I said.

"Oh, poor baby," I told him and patted his arm.

LaDainian looked nervous. "You don't like it?"

"No, no. It's beautiful," I said.

"Mama, you look like you're on crack," Londria said, still laughing.

"Londria," I said, "it's a picture, a tattooed picture. Okay? Come on. Give him a break."

"I'm just saying," she said with a smirk.

LaDainian ignored her. But thankfully, he got the spelling fixed. That's my kid. He has a heart as big as Texas.

|||

Dainian's sophomore football season turned out to be much better than he had anticipated. Coach Fran moved him into the running back position, and Dainian worked harder than ever to prove that he had made the right decision. The team was also doing better than the previous season. By the end of his sophomore year, Dainian had more than seven hundred yards—and that's a lot for playing backup to starting running back Basil Mitchell.

The team had a tremendous amount of enthusiasm and talent. And even though they only won six or seven games that year, it was enough to take them to a bowl game in El Paso.

When we went to El Paso to play the University of Southern California in the Sun Bowl, we were the underdogs. All the predictions said that we would lose by a large margin. And when we took the field, there was very little purple in the stands.

But LaDainian played well in that game. I think he got close to a hundred yards. And in spite of our underdog status, we won! That 1998 win was the first victory in a bowl game for TCU in forty-one years. LaDainian was thrilled to be part of that victory.

|||

His sophomore year may have been good, but his junior year was a huge success. Finally he was starting running back, and he had a very good run. Other than a few bumps and bruises, he had no major injuries.

The most amazing part was to see how famous my son

became. In two years' time, everybody seemed to know his name. Sportscasters all over the country were talking about him. He was appearing in national papers and magazines.

Because of his many setbacks, Dainian had not yet been able to show how talented he really was. But when he finally got the chance, he exploded onto the national football stage.

Many times when a kid gains that instant celebrity status, he can't handle it. I often read about these young men who get into trouble—drinking and driving, using drugs, mouthing off, allowing their fame to go to their heads. But I was proud to see that never happened with LaDainian. He handled the attention the same way he handled everything else in his life: with humility and grace. I was overjoyed to watch him give honor to the fans who wrangled for his autograph or simply wanted his attention. He was always kind and respectful. I was proud that he remained focused and humble.

|||

At the game against UTEP (University of Texas at El Paso) that year, LaDainian ran 406 yards and made six touchdowns.

Unfortunately, I wasn't able to attend that game. LaVar's high school team was in a play-off game that same day. LaVar played defensive tackle. Normally we didn't have scheduling conflicts because the high school games were on Fridays and the college games were on Saturdays. But Herman and I decided to attend LaVar's game while I listened to LaDainian's game on a radio that was plugged into my ear.

So there I sat in the bleachers watching LaVar's team lose as I listened to LaDainian's team win. When I say that LaVar's team was losing, I'm being kind. The other team was mopping the floor with our boys, and the supporters in the stands were watching our hopes for a championship title being dashed.

I felt so terrible for LaVar! I knew that those players on the field were doing everything they could and that they probably felt awful. But I also knew that while LaVar wasn't thrilled to be losing, he would take it in stride. To him, football was just a game. It wasn't "do or die" like it was to Dainian. By that point in LaVar's life, he was much more interested in poetry and writing than sports.

So while sitting in this crowd of heartbroken fans, I was listening to the radio sportscaster shout in my ear that Dainian had crossed into the end zone and scored a touchdown. I leaped to my feet, arms waving, and screamed, "Yea!" at the top of my voice. Heads turned and glared at me because I had just celebrated as the opposing team was killing us.

No sooner had I offered my apologies to the angry crowd and taken my seat, than the radio announcer listed something else spectacular that LaDainian had done and I was back on my feet screaming again. This time the crowd didn't seem as forgiving. Once again I muttered, "Sorry."

My nephews, who had come to the play-off game with me, turned and asked, "Auntie, what's LaDainian doing? What's going on in his game?"

Try as I might, I couldn't keep my emotions under control, and I finally told the crowd what was going on in my ear. I hoped they might understand and perhaps share my enthusiasm when they heard that my older son had scored six touchdowns and rushed for 406 yards.

But realistically, being a seasoned football mom, I knew that they didn't care if the sweet Lord Jesus was whispering in my ear; I needed to be quiet and respectful of their emotions and to the team on the field. Poor LaVar—he felt bad. That was the first round of play-offs, and they lost. As soon as the final score popped onto the scoreboard, I rushed out of my seat and down to the field to comfort him and the other players.

At the end of LaDainian's junior year, TCU went to the Mobile

Alabama Bowl, where they played East Carolina. My nephew had a Chevy Suburban, and we all packed into it for the trip. We had so much fun! But it was so cold there. We had to find earmuffs and boots and even went out and bought gloves.

Once there, we stood in a crowd that was a mixture of supporters from the two teams. I overheard fans from the opposing team talking about how they were going to stop that running back LaDainian Tomlinson. This was nothing new. It seemed as though every game we went to, no matter what our record was, win or lose, there was always someone boasting at the top of his voice about how their team was going to stop my son. They would go on and on about how their team was going to do this or that. I would always think, *Okay, big talker, we'll see. Time will tell.* And time and again we would dominate the field. I'm a football mom, so I can say that!

This bowl game in Alabama wasn't any different. I ran into a family who had a son on the opposing team. They knew who I was and they were very kind, telling me that LaDainian was an outstanding running back. But then the father proceeded to tell me all the reasons LaDainian wouldn't make it past their team.

"There's no way for him to get past our boys this time," he told me.

"Oh, really?" I said, having a bit of fun. "Okay, well, may the best man win."

I left it at that, because I didn't know what was going to happen when the teams hit the field. But with the stats LaDainian was racking up, I didn't *need* to say anything. My son's actions on the field spoke louder than any smart comment I could make.

TCU won that game, and LaDainian posted a few records. The 406 yards he ran against UTEP were a 1999 NCAA record for yards rushed in a game. And he ended the year leading the NCAA with 1,850 yards rushing and eighteen touchdowns. I may be biased toward my son, but I do believe the best man won.

CHAPTER 15

"I've Met Someone"

WHEN LADAINIAN WAS TWELVE years old, he once entered the
kitchen looking sad and dejected. He stood at the kitchen counter and rested his head on his arms.

"What's the matter, Dainian?" I asked.

"I'm never going to have a girlfriend," he said.

"What? Why do you think that?" I had noticed that LaDainian's
friends had begun to pay attention to girls. They were always pulling some girl's hair and giggling or pinching them and running.
"Why do you think you'll never have a girlfriend?"

"Because I'm so ugly!" he snapped.

His words broke my heart. "Son, you are not ugly! You are a
very handsome young man."

"I am?" he questioned as he lifted his head, smiling.

"Yes, you are a very good-looking boy! You look just like your
daddy, and I married your daddy. But don't you worry about
that right now. God is going to send you the right girl at the right
time. Until then, all you have to do is be the best kid you can be.
I'm real proud of you."

"Okay, Mama."

I gave him a hug and a kiss. Then he left the room with a huge
smile on his face and perhaps some newfound confidence.

I'm not sure where he got the idea that he was ugly, unless some little girl had told him that. But I knew from this conversation that my son was growing up and that sports might actually have some competition for his attention.

Early in his junior year at Texas Christian University, he broke up with a young lady he had been dating since high school. That was a difficult decision for him, because he really liked her—we all did. But he just felt that it wasn't the right relationship for him to continue. Although I was sad to hear about the breakup, I trusted him to make the right decision because I knew he was serious about the relationships he entered.

Then around Easter, he called and said he was coming over and was going to bring someone with him. I figured it was a group of guys. He often brought friends over for a big holiday meal, especially if the boys couldn't go home to be with their own families.

When he arrived, he entered the house wearing that big smile of his.

"Mama, I have someone I want you to meet." And in walked a beautiful, tall young lady with shoulder-length black hair and brown eyes. "This is Torsha."

She smiled widely. What struck me most about her was that she reminded me of our family. She wasn't hanging back like she was shy; she was quick to smile and seemed very genuine.

"Hi," I said and gave her a hug. I wasn't expecting this! I was still almost looking around for the group of guys!

"You're a beautiful young lady," I told her, glancing over at Dainian, who seemed nervous about the whole situation.

"Come on in!" I said and escorted her to our living room. We sat and chatted briefly. I noticed Dainian never left the room the entire time.

He had seen her on campus, and apparently he watched her for two months to see what kind of girl she was. Then he told a friend he wanted to meet her. As he explained this, I figured, *Okay, you all are together. So let's look to the future of where this relationship is headed.* As we chatted, I tried to figure out what kind of character she had, how she intended to treat my son— all the protective motherly concerns! My son was special and I treated him special, so I expected the other woman in his life to do the same.

I found out Torsha was a freshman. Her grandfather was a pastor (that got bonus points, since I knew she was raised in a good, God-fearing home). She was a strong Christian who loved the Lord. And not only was she beautiful, she was intelligent. She was a Bill Gates Millennium Scholar who carried a 4.0 average.

If there's one thing about LaDainian: he is attracted to brains as much as he is to beauty. It must be because of how hard he had to study in school. I don't think he realizes that if his knowledge of football was tested he would be at the top of his class.

Torsha admitted that she didn't know who LaDainian was when they first met. If she had, she might never have gone out with him because her daddy had warned her to stay away from football players. She hadn't been caught up in all the hype like others on campus were.

What really won me over was when she said, "I know you and LaDainian have a good relationship. I've always wanted a man who knows how to treat his mom, because if he knows how to treat his mom he knows how to treat me."

I thought, *This is a mature-minded individual.*

"Well, he definitely knows how to treat women," I told her proudly. "I taught both my boys how to respect women."

I thought back to the rules I had when the kids were growing up. Respect was on the top of the list when I talked to LaDainian about his relationships with women. It was important for him to put their wants and needs before his own. But I also told him, "If a girl cares for you, she will not take advantage of that, and she'll consider the things that are important to you, too. If two people in a relationship will put God first and the needs of each another ahead of their own, they can achieve a wonderful balance and have a strong, good relationship."

LaDainian had been invited to prom when he was a sophomore in high school. When he was ready to go, I gave him twenty-five dollars and said, "LaDainian, when you take her to eat, you make sure that she eats, even if you don't."

When he came back home, I asked him how it went.

"Fine," he said and laughed. "I had enough for a little something."

I told him I was sorry I hadn't been able to give him more money. He told me not to worry, that the girl was happy and he just appreciated me for all I had done for him.

Now as I looked across the room at Torsha, I knew that if LaDainian thought enough of her to bring her home to meet me, she must be someone very special. And that's when I knew she would probably become his wife. Dainian didn't go through a lot of girlfriends; he never dated just to date. He was a "one-woman man," and he had always said that he was dating to find a life partner, not just to have a good time.

But still, somewhere in the back of my mind I couldn't help but worry just a little. After all, he had been with his previous girlfriend for five years. And if that relationship wasn't truly over, I didn't want LaDainian to bring any of that baggage into this relationship.

Later that week LaDainian called me and asked, "What do you think of Torsha?"

"I think she's sweet," I told him truthfully.

The more I got to know her, the more I began to believe that she was the one for him. So I began to pray for both of them, that they would make the right decisions for each other and that they would honor God through their relationship.

||||

Having LaDainian at TCU and LaVar on the Garland High School team kept football in the center of our lives. And as LaDainian grew as a football player, I found myself making some personal improvements of my own. I returned to school, obtained my real estate license, and began to make a pretty good living selling houses. Also, as an ordained minister, I began to work with several churches in the area, including my own in Garland. Unfortunately, during this period, my marriage to Herman also began to unravel.

I always thought that Herman was one of the finest people on this earth. The love and support he gave my family and me were lifesaving. When he entered our lives, the kids and I went from day-to-day survival to a secure and happy life. Not only did he help us financially, he also gave us his time. He sat beside me at most of the kids' activities and sometimes sat alone when I couldn't attend. But after twelve years of marriage and much deliberation, I found myself in divorce court once again.

Some of the problems had been out of my control. Herman had a passion for smoking, drinking, and eating fried foods that led to a stroke. I nursed him through his recovery, and God raised him up and healed him. You could not even tell he had had a stroke. But the doctor warned Herman that his arteries were so clogged that very little oxygen was getting to his brain.

"Mr. Chappell," he said, "I don't see how your brain is getting oxygen, but it is. And your arteries are so clogged we need to go in and open them up. In fact, I'm amazed that you are walking around, working, and leading a normal life in this condition. But you're pressing your luck. You need to make some serious changes."

The first step was for Herman to go on a strict diet. This was extremely difficult for him because he loved his fried foods. If something sat still long enough, he would dip it in flour and chicken-fry it. I moved into mother mode and tried to get Herman to follow the doctor's orders of no smoking, drinking, or eating fatty foods. When I felt that I was talking to a brick wall and my nagging was just making things worse, I confronted Herman and asked him if he was trying to kill himself.

He agreed to go to the hospital to have his arteries cleared, but while he was lying on the table waiting for the surgery, he had a seizure. So he left without the procedure and said he would never go back.

He continued to live his destructive lifestyle. When I confronted him about it, he would say, "I'm an adult. I can do what I want."

During this time Herman's drinking grew worse, and he became verbally abusive. I often left the room to avoid a confrontation, but he would follow me and continue to berate me. He didn't feel that I was paying him enough attention. It seemed that one of his biggest concerns was that I was attending church without him. He was afraid that I was interested in another man.

I told him that if he was tired of seeing his wife put on her finest and go out the door without him, he should join me. This was my attempt at getting him in the church, where I hoped he would find the help from the Lord that he so desperately needed. Sometimes he would come, be moved by the Spirit, and cry. On the way home he would promise to quit drinking and to start eating right, but it never lasted.

Then he started to leave for several days at a time. He always came back laughing and making light of it. He would ask me if I was mad. This went on for a while until one day he came home, packed his bags, and left.

I had no idea where he went, but I wondered if he was having an affair. I began to pray, "Lord, what do I do? What kind of role model is this for my sons?"

A week later he called, crying, and asked if he could come back. He promised to follow his doctor's orders and quit drinking. I told him that we could try again under those circumstances. Unfortunately, it was only a matter of days before he was drunk and arguing with me again. This time, though, he took the verbal abuse to a higher and louder level.

All at once he raised his hand as if he was going to hit me. Out of nowhere, six-foot-three LaVar came flying over me from behind, caught Herman's hand in midair, and slammed him against the wall.

I was terrified, because I didn't want LaVar to kill Herman and end up in jail. Finally, I was able to pull my younger son off him. LaVar stormed into his room and slammed the door. Then I turned to Herman and told him to leave. We couldn't have this behavior in our home. Herman had become too unpredictable.

I didn't want to get a divorce. I didn't want my kids to go through that again. But eight months later, I discovered Herman was involved with another woman. At that point I felt God free me to pursue a divorce. The whole situation saddened me deeply.

For the first time, LaVar and I found ourselves truly alone. And financially, times were as desperate as they had ever been. I don't know how we made it. There was a period when it seemed I couldn't sell a house if one fell on me. I might have five contracts lined up, and one by one they would fall through.

I was consumed with fear and worry because things were not coming together. With one son in college and another in high school, I just didn't see how we were going to make it.

The phone seemed to be ringing off the wall with creditors and threats. I would get so depressed listening to them that I wanted to cry. Then one day the Lord told me, *Why do you sit and listen to all the bad things these people are saying to you? They're calling on the phone that you pay for, threatening you, and putting you in a depressed mood. You don't need to be told that a bill hasn't been paid—you're the first one to know that.*

So once I knew what the person on the phone wanted, I was not rude; I simply laid down the phone on the table until the caller hung up. That was the most liberating thing I have ever done.

Eventually my spirits began to lift even though my circumstances hadn't changed. God was telling me to get control over my emotions and be strong.

One day I was sitting in a chair reading my Bible. I put it down on my lap and began watching the blackbirds out the window. They were picking through the grass looking for seeds and bugs.

They are scavengers, the Lord reminded me. *I feed them. You will never have to search for your food because I will provide it for you. When it gets bad and you can't see a way out, just lean on Me. I know where I am taking you.*

My faith grew that day. LaVar and I might not have had all the things we wanted, but we had food. God took care of us. And when we were at our lowest and our water was turned off, a Christian ministry showed up and helped us pay the bill. The water was off and then on again in a matter of hours without my children having to know.

I don't know how we did it. But by God's grace and goodness, I never felt alone or afraid, and I learned to trust in Him as my provider. When a number of real estate deals finally came through, I was able to get back on my feet and start over. I felt like Job: doubly blessed after losing so much.

CHAPTER 16

The Heisman Trophy

AS LADAINIAN STARTED his senior year at TCU, I began to understand how Dorothy in *The Wizard of Oz* must have felt. We were both little country girls who were caught up in a whirl-wind that dropped us in a colorful, magical land. But instead of Munchkins, I was surrounded by six-foot Horned Frogs. And there was no yellow brick road in this place; it was a deep shade of purple all the way.

Coming off the glow of LaDainian's junior year, we were pumped and ready to get the ball rolling for this final run. Fort Worth had embraced my son, and the atmosphere at TCU was electric as talks of a Heisman Trophy for him swirled.

In fact, one fan in particular seemed to have started the begin-ning of the frenzy. At the end of LaDainian's junior year, some-one made a bumper sticker that said "LT for Heisman." Nobody had ever called LaDainian "LT" before. Now it was everywhere!

Every game I went to, I could hear the crowds chanting, "LT! LT! LT!" It was amazing to hear their voices and think, *That's my son! They're cheering for my son!* It felt like a dream. I wanted to jump out of my seat and go parading onto the field, arms high in the air, yelling, "That's my boy! My baby LaDainian!"

While I was caught up in the excitement, I was surprised to

find my role shifting from number-one fan to business manager and publicist. It seemed that every other day I was needed for an interview or signature for contracts for promotions, insurance, and the like, since he was still under twenty-one. Agents had begun to contact LaDainian, and we knew he needed one to negotiate with the NFL. Over and over I would look at my boy and think, *You're doing it. You're really doing it.* I was so proud. And he had known it all the time.

|||

By this point, LaVar was ready to leave for college, and I was spending more and more time driving between Garland and Fort Worth to help LaDainian in his business dealings. So I decided to move to Fort Worth to be closer to LaDainian for his senior year. I relocated to a comfortable, tree-filled neighborhood called Eastern Hills in Fort Worth, about five miles from the campus.

One evening I was sitting in the house watching television when I noticed a commercial for football. LaDainian's life seemed on track with his dreams and goals. But the more I thought about it, I realized that it wasn't *quite* where it should be. He needed his dad. The entire time LaDainian had played football, while he was working hard and receiving all those accolades for breaking records, Tee had never once come to watch his son play. Not even when LaDainian was in Pop Warner league. It broke my heart. And I wondered: if it was breaking *my* heart, what must it be doing to LaDainian's?

I looked around my house. It was large and offered plenty of extra room, more than I could ever fill. The way the house was arranged, I could easily have a guest or roommate and offer him or her complete privacy. Each bedroom had its own bath and was separated by a large family room.

Was it time to try to reconcile with Tee once more? God had

blessed me so much, and Dainian needed his father. The least I could do was reach out and offer this once-in-a-lifetime experience to Tee.

I began to argue within myself. *No,* I thought, *that's just too weird. Inviting my ex-husband to live with me? What would people think?* But the more I thought it over, the more I realized I couldn't be completely happy watching LaDainian fulfill his dreams without the one man by my side who had given him the love of football in the first place.

I decided not to say anything to Dainian, though, in case things didn't work out. I didn't want him to get his hopes up.

So I called Tee to run the idea past him, half expecting him to scoff but hoping he would agree for his son's sake.

Tee was thrilled.

"'Course I'll come!" he said. "He's my son. I've gotta see him play."

We made arrangements for me to drive down to Tomlinson Hill, pick him up, and bring him back to Fort Worth. We moved him into the house just in time to make it to our son's first home game.

I knew I had to tell LaDainian so he could get Tee a ticket, but I told him it was "just in case." That day Tee and I drove to the stadium and took our seats. I was so excited! We sat together like two old friends, talking and laughing. It felt wonderful.

Before every game, LaDainian had the habit of looking into the stands to see where I was sitting. Our simple eye contact said it all. Love and support passed between us, and it seemed that the crowd was gone and we were alone for that second.

This time when he looked for me, he also caught sight of his dad sitting next to me. LaDainian stopped dead in his tracks and stared, his eyes big as saucers. In that moment, I saw my son not as a five-foot-ten-and-a-half-inch, 225-pound man but as a little boy. In my eyes, LaDainian was five years old again, trying to please his father. My mind raced through the memories: the first fish he'd caught and how excited he was to tell Tee, the way he loved to watch the Dallas Cowboys with his dad, the sound of the two of them playing catch in our backyard. My eyes filled with tears, and I noticed that LaDainian blinked several times to keep his tears at bay too.

One of the other players called his name, and the connection was gone. Dainian had to go back to the business at hand: winning this football game.

Throughout the game, Tee and I cheered and reminisced. Tee was so proud of his son; he nodded and smiled through the entire game. Of course, TCU won, even though LaDainian said it was a terrible game for him, since he gained only seventy-five yards on twenty-one carries.

After the game, my son the football star went straight to his father and broke down. Tee kept saying how proud he was of him and what a good job he had done. The two talked, and I think Dainian made some peace with the past—at least as much as he could in that short time. I knew there were too many years of hurt and frustration to be erased in one meeting, but at least it was a start.

Dainian seemed pleased to hear that Tee was staying with me and would be attending all the home games with me. Dainian wanted to spend more time with his dad, but he was so busy with football practice and studies that he simply couldn't get away. So he always joined us for a meal after the home games. And he called whenever he could to talk to his father.

Tee and I were like roommates and didn't bother each other. He was on his best behavior and seemed to do well with his use of prescription medication.

He often walked around the neighborhood and told anyone who would listen about his son who was going to put TCU on the map. Then he would brag about the UTEP game and

LaDainian's six touchdowns and 406 yards rushing. Beaming with pride, he loved to talk about the Heisman run.

Thankfully, TCU had an amazing season and gave Tee plenty to brag about. That year LaDainian led the NCAA by racking up 2,158 yards rushing. He made twenty-two touchdowns and 354 yards receiving. LaDainian kept saying, "It wasn't all me. I had a lot of help. The entire offensive line should get credit too!" His offensive line was comprised of Jeff Millican, David Bobo, Michael Keathley, Victor Payne, and Jeff Garner, who were affectionately called "the big uglies."

But even though Tee loved every minute of the action, I suspected that he had not completely kicked his addiction. We bought him a good used truck so he could run back and forth to Tomlinson Hill and take care of his business. I don't know what he did while he was there, and I didn't want to know. He began to stay down there during the week but fortunately always made it back in time to go to LaDainian's game. For that I am grateful.

Tee had given Dainian a love of the game that changed the history books. When LaDainian completed his college career, he had 5,263 rushing yards, which earned him sixth place in the history books of the NCAA Division I.

||

That year TCU went back to the Mobile Alabama Bowl, where they played Southern Mississippi. This time, though, it was without our head coach.

After Coach Fran had done such a remarkable job building the football program at TCU, he took the job as head coach in Alabama. When he told the athletic staff at TCU that he had accepted this position, they immediately released him. Unfortunately, it was before he had the chance to coach that last bowl game. And I think his absence cost our team the game.

Our boys suffered a heartbreaking loss without their coach. LaDainian's last college game ended up with a stroke in the loss column. Still, I think that Coach Fran did more for the TCU football program than anyone had done in a long time. Eight members from LaDainian's team were invited to attend the NFL Scouting Combines, which is a lot! Most teams get to send only one or two boys.

For LaDainian, though, Coach Fran's dismissal was especially difficult. When the coach first arrived and moved Dainian to fullback, Dainian wasn't sure he was going to like the coach *at all*. But Coach Fran became a mentor to LaDainian. For that, he will always hold a special place in my heart, and I know in LaDainian's as well.

As soon as the bowl games were finished, Dainian's agent pulled Dainian out of his last semester of school to send him to a training camp in Florida to prepare for combines. Although I wasn't thrilled that he wasn't going to complete his college education, I knew school was important enough to him that he would eventually go back and finish what he started.

|||

Award season begins after football season is over, and LaDainian was showered with praise and awards. He received the prestigious Doak Walker Award. Named after the SMU and Detroit Lions football player, this award honors the country's best college running back. The Walker family hosts this award every year in memory of their father, one of the best athletes in the history of the sport.

Unfortunately, LaDainian couldn't attend every award ceremony. Usually, I simply sat in the crowd and beamed as others applauded my son, but one day I was tapped on the shoulder and asked to accept an award for him. The Dallas

Athletic Club was presenting awards, and LaDainian was in
Florida at training camp.

I was used to speaking in public, but I wasn't used to getting up
in front of a crowd this big. I looked out at the sea of what seemed
like a thousand people and gulped—I wasn't so sure about this!

The host relocated my seat up onstage, where I sat next to
Lamar Hunt, owner of the Kansas City Chiefs and a well-known
entrepreneur. I didn't even know who he was at the time, but
we chatted and laughed easily. Not until later did someone tell
me who he was. He made me feel at ease and almost helped me
forget that I was going to have to give a speech. I looked around
at the others sitting on stage with us. Dallas mayor Ron Kirk and
other dignitaries were there, as well as several representatives
from the Dallas Mavericks and the Cowboys. And then I spotted
Emmitt Smith. I smiled.

This is fitting, I thought. *Here's the man who fueled my son's
dream when he was a child.*

When it was my turn to speak, many of the players onstage
reached out and patted my arm as I walked by them.

"You'll do great, Mom" and "Go get 'em, Mom," they said.
Once again I was reminded that as a football mother, you
become a mother to all the boys on the team and they become
your sons. As much as I yearned for my own son to be there,
I found comfort in the words of those who were.

Although I don't remember much of what I said, I do remember that I thanked Dallas and Fort Worth for embracing my son.
I accepted the award and explained why LaDainian couldn't be
there in person. I was just glad when it was over. I was afraid my
knocking knees were making more noise than my voice was!

After the presentation, a couple congratulated me and asked
me something I had never been asked before: "How did you raise
a champion?"

The question threw me but pleased me at the same time.

While I was talking to them, a man walked up beside me and waited patiently for me to finish. When I turned to him, I realized that he was Ross Perot! He clasped my hand with both of his.

"I wanted to congratulate you on the wonderful job you did with your son."

It turned out he was a fan of Dainian's.

He made the most wonderful impression on me. There he stood, one of the most powerful men in the country, waiting for me to finish my conversation so he could congratulate me. Never have I seen such a gracious gentleman.

But while every award is special and deeply appreciated, one in particular is so coveted and prestigious in the sports world that even a *nomination* can cause a frenzy. The Heisman Trophy is awarded to the most outstanding player in college football.

When LaDainian received the nomination, not only did the TCU community celebrate, but the entire city of Fort Worth went crazy! They painted the town purple. Everywhere I looked I saw men, women, and children wearing LaDainian's number 5 jersey. "LT for Heisman" was plastered on bumper stickers and banners throughout Fort Worth, Dallas, and the surrounding areas.

What was most shocking to me, though, was the first time I drove down the street and saw a twenty-foot picture of my son's smiling face staring down at me from a billboard. I almost drove straight off the road while I shoved my face as far into the windshield as I could and gaped.

The banners and posters and bumper stickers and shirts were one thing. But they didn't make everything feel as real as seeing my son's photo plastered across billboards all over the city. I just couldn't get used to it!

"Did you know about the billboards?" I asked LaDainian after I saw the first one.

"Oh, yeah," he said nonchalantly.

"Why didn't you tell me? This is a big deal!"

He just shrugged. "Aw, mom," he said, looking embarrassed.

I found myself scoping out the billboards—which wasn't too difficult since they seemed to be everywhere—and driving by them just to see LaDainian. I'd gawk and smile and think, *That's my son.* And every time I don't know how I kept my car in its lane. It's a wonder I didn't get into any accidents.

That boy was swamped with interviews and photo shoots, and as the hoopla continued, we received word that LaDainian was one of the top four in the running for the award.

The Heisman representatives contacted us to make plans for LaDainian to go to New York City, where the results would be announced in early December. During the conversation they suggested that I attend too. Although I would have loved to go, money was too tight, so I didn't even dream of it.

When some friends discovered that I would have to pass up this once-in-a-lifetime opportunity because of finances, they chipped in and surprised me with a round-trip ticket to New York City. And before I knew it, it was December, and I was on a plane to meet my son, who had flown in early to do media interviews and photo shoots.

A Heisman representative picked me up at the airport the morning of the ceremony and drove me to the hotel where everyone was staying. My first impression of New York was mass confusion. There wasn't a square inch that wasn't filled with something. Everywhere I looked there were people and skyscrapers—and the noise was unbelievable! With all the cars honking and people yelling, I could hardly hear myself think.

I got settled into the hotel, then LaDainian called me, and we went out to eat. I was looking forward to spending time with him. We talked about who we thought would win and the accomplishments of all the finalists. Of course, I was hopeful LaDainian was going to win.

After the meal, we went back to the hotel to rest and get ready for the evening.

The ceremony was formal, so I borrowed a suit from my sister Theopal, and LaDainian rented a tuxedo. He looked so handsome! When the time came for the ceremony, a well-dressed gentleman in a dark luxury car picked us up at the hotel. As the driver approached a street he was going to turn onto, he spoke into a phone and said, "I'm turning onto such and such street, and I have LT."

As soon as we made the turn onto that street, it was deserted. There wasn't a man, woman, child, dog, cat, or rat in sight. There were no car doors opening or closing. There was no action at all. It seemed like the air wasn't even moving. It was weird—like one of those horror movies where the town is empty and you don't know where everyone has disappeared to. I've seen more action in downtown Marlin after midnight.

The event was being held at the Downtown Athletic Club, and when we arrived there we were ushered into a holding room, where we were to meet, greet, and interview.

Inside, there were tables filled with food. As we checked out the fare, LaDainian leaned over and whispered to me, "Mama, how many ways can you fix a chicken? I've been here two days, and every time I turn around someone is giving me chicken. I think it may be the *same* chicken!"

We laughed. It seemed to break some of the nervousness I was feeling. As they began to seat people in the main room, a man approached and informed us that we were to have bodyguards. LaDainian would have four, and although I was surprised, I could understand the need. But when the man assigned two bodyguards for me, I was floored! Why in the world would I need bodyguards? But the men were big and serious and focused on doing their jobs, so I went along with it.

When I entered the room, I was delighted to discover that

Coach Fran and his wife had flown in from Alabama for the event. The four nominees were seated together at a long table at the front: Chris Weinke, a quarterback from Florida State; Josh Heupel, a quarterback out of Oklahoma; Drew Brees, the talented Purdue quarterback; and LaDainian, the only running back up for the prize.

The four were seated with Chris first, Josh second, Drew third, and LaDainian fourth. I was struck by the age difference in the nominees. Chris Weinke was twenty-eight and had played minor league baseball for six years before he returned to college to play football for Florida State. The others were between twenty-one and twenty-two years old.

When Chris Weinke was announced the winner, my boy was the first to jump out of his seat on the end and run to congratulate him. That show of sportsmanship made me as proud as if he had won. And you know, even though LaDainian and Drew Brees came in last and next to last, those two have had hugely successful careers in the NFL. With the Doak Walker Award and Heisman publicity under his belt, LaDainian faced the upcoming NFL draft with optimism. But before LaDainian went to the draft, he had to face the combines.

Not everyone knows about combines—the NFL Scouting Combine or National Invitational Camp. Some have called the combines a "meat market" because the emphasis is on the man's physical and psychological condition, as many tests are performed. But basically it's an invitation-only job fair for the NFL.

During what would have been LaDainian's second semester as a senior, in February 2000, he and three hundred other prospective NFL players traveled to the RCA Dome in Indianapolis for the better part of a week.

I went to the airport with LaDainian to send him off to these legendary combines, and while we were there, he introduced me to one of his friends.

"Hey, Mom," LaDainian said, "this is Leonard Davis. He's going to the combines too."

This guy was a six-foot-six, 365-pound giant of a man. Dainian looked like a midget next to him. I nearly fainted. I thought the guys were big in college. Was this the size of the men who would be hitting my child in the pros?

"Please tell me you're not going to be tackling my baby!" I said.

"No, Mom, he's an offensive tackle," LaDainian answered for him.

As I looked at Davis. my mind was screaming to Dainian, *Quit now, baby, while there's time. Please, quit!*

But I knew there was no way he was going to quit now. He was too close.

In Indianapolis, Dainian underwent a series of drills, tests, and interviews with NFL personnel. He met with head coaches, general managers, scouts, and medical experts from all thirty-one NFL teams (Houston came in the following year), and they evaluated his eligibility for the upcoming draft.

La Dainian said they poked and prodded and checked every part of his body, including his teeth. They wanted to see if they could spot any condition that might interfere with his football performance. And there was no room for modesty. While many of the tests were performed with the men in their underwear, the dress code for the drug test was a birthday suit.

The last day he was at the combines, he called me.

"Mom, I blew 'em out. I blew 'em out!"

"Great, Son! That's really good!"

He ran forty yards in 4.38 seconds—Deion Sanders ran a 4.2. He had impressed them and he knew it.

After the combines, the only thing standing between LaDainian and the pros was the draft. And that's where he headed next.

PART FOUR

NFL

CHAPTER 17

The Draft

IT WAS APRIL, and we were off to New York City again—this time for something much bigger than the Heisman. This time we were going to get LaDainian a job.

Players who are expected to be picked in the first rounds of the draft are usually invited to New York to be on hand for the action. Our small group went for this honor—LaDainian, LaVar, Londria, my nephew André, Torsha, and me. We stayed at a hotel, W, with the magical motto "Whatever/Whenever," which was situated not too far from Madison Square Garden, where the draft picks would be announced and televised.

A number of players were staying at the same hotel we were, including Michael Vick and Leonard Davis, the massive man I'd met when LaDainian was going to the combines. We thought our motley crew of six people was a lot. But Leonard was from a small town in Texas about the size of Tomlinson Hill, and he brought twenty-seven people with him for support.

The atmosphere at the Madison Square Garden was electric. This was one of the biggest days in these players' lives. Their futures and careers would be determined here. One of the groups that was recruiting there was the Professional Football Players Mothers' Association (PFPMA). This nonprofit organization provides information, helps with their sons' charities, and holds fund-raisers, among other things.

They have a mothers' association, I thought, impressed. I had never heard of such a thing!

The draft can go on for several days, but since we assumed LaDainian was going to be drafted in one of the early rounds— at least we hoped—we arrived at the hall early. A representative met us and escorted us to a large holding room, where we were to wait until our player's name was called.

We were pleased to spot Drew Brees with his family. We reconnected a bit, talking more about the Heisman and the draft picks, and then we grabbed some seats and looked around. The room was filling with players and their families, looking nervous and excited.

Tables filled with snacks and beverages lined the walls throughout the room. And there were televisions everywhere! The draft is televised, so sports commentators were analyzing and guessing what teams would take which players and why. Our ears perked up when one of the commentators mentioned Dainian's name.

"He's too small," one sportscaster said, shaking his head. They felt Deuce McAllister was a better pick. Deuce was bigger and from a better-known school.

"Don't listen to them, Dainian," I said, more for my sake than his. I knew he wasn't concerned about it. He had already made it this far! Once the draft began, speakers in our room projected what was happening in another room, where all the NFL team executives were making decisions, trades, and deals. San Diego had first pick. We held our breath, waiting to hear the Chargers' choice. We knew from the combines that they might be interested in Dainian. And they were Dainian's first choice.

"San Diego gives up first pick with Atlanta for a trade," the voice announced.

"What does that mean?" I asked.

It turned out that San Diego traded places with Atlanta so that the Falcons could get their first pick. By doing so, San Diego got a sweeter deal by getting two additional players. I didn't follow it all; I just knew that now San Diego would be the fifth team to choose. It was tough to keep up with all the complicated rules they were following.

I prayed silently that nobody else would choose Dainian before it was San Diego's turn.

"Mom," LaDainian said, "if San Diego doesn't pick me, I just don't know—"

"It's out of our hands, baby," I told him. "God will provide."

Atlanta picked Michael Vick for quarterback. The crowd cheered, and Michael and his family got up from their chairs and walked out of the room. We watched on the television as he and his entourage stepped onto the big stage and received a Falcons jersey and cap.

Then it was Arizona's turn. Dainian shook his head again— too hot and dry. We knew we shouldn't be picky since he was being drafted into the pros, but we could dream!

Next it was the Ohio teams: the Browns and the Bengals. Dainian shook his head. "I don't want to go there. Ohio's too cold." We all agreed.

Finally, after we'd been sitting there for more than an hour and a half, San Diego's turn rolled around.

Paul Tagliabue, the NFL commissioner, took the microphone and announced, "San Diego chooses LaDainian Tomlinson." We jumped to our feet and whooped and hollered. He was the first running back to be drafted.

Oh, my goodness, I realized. *If San Diego had kept their place, my son would have been the very first draft pick. But fifth was certainly nothing to be ashamed of either!*

We grabbed our belongings and headed toward the doorway.

An escort met us there and led us down a short hallway and onto the large stage. Cameras and people were everywhere. Paul Tagliabue greeted us onstage and handed LaDainian a Chargers ball cap and a jersey with a big number one on them.

After a few moments of congratulations, the escort motioned for everybody but Dainian to leave the stage so he could have his photo taken with the NFL commissioner. He was congratulated and then he shook hands with the commissioner before donning his cap and holding up his jersey for the photo.

He made it, I realized, feeling overwhelmed with emotion. *He really made it.*

Not only had he just been drafted into professional football by his number-one choice, he would also be the starting running back! No more working for two or three years to earn that spot; it was his from the get-go. He was going to begin playing professionally that same year.

We left Dainian and went into another large room—this one for the media—to wait until Dainian came in to do his first official NFL interviews with the press. As we walked in, I couldn't believe my eyes. Michael Vick was still at the microphone answering questions! That meant LaDainian wouldn't do his interview until they finished with Michael and the other three players. We settled into our seats, knowing this was going to take a while!

Finally LaDainian entered the room, wearing his dark blue jersey and cap with the lightning bolt splashed across them, and stepped up to the microphone. He's shy, so I knew he was feeling nervous about so much attention. He said he was happy to be going to San Diego and really appreciated this opportunity to be able to do the thing he loved at a professional level.

As I sat listening to him answer questions, I was suddenly overcome with emotion again.

"Thank You, God," I whispered over and over. "Thank You for

this blessing. Thank You for keeping Your promises and for taking care of my son."

Then it hit me: my son had just become a millionaire. I had never thought about it before, because I was always more concerned that he just get a job! Our family had gone through periods of near poverty and pain. And my son was never going to have to experience that again. He would never again have to worry that his jeans might shrink before he could afford another pair or eat only noodles.

I reached down to my purse and patted it. Inside was LaDainian's letter he had written to me back in high school. I kept it with me everywhere I went. He had meant those words when he wrote them. Now they had all come true.

After his interviews were finished, Dainian rejoined us and another escort took us to a different room, this one sponsored by ESPN. As we were walking, LaDainian leaned over to me and whispered, "We made it, Mom. We made it! I believe I can run with the big boys now."

Inside the room were more tables of food, and we mingled with the other players' families. We saw Leonard with what seemed like his entire town. Even the commentators made remarks about the size of his entourage.

We saw Drew Brees again. He was the number thirty-two draft pick, and San Diego got him. We were all thrilled—he was a good kid, and he and Dainian became fast friends. I was pleased that Dainian would know another rookie on the team. They would be able to lean on each other during that first year.

We stayed in that room for the rest of the day, heading back to the hotel around eight o'clock. Everyone but LaDainian was set to leave New York the next day. He would stay another day to talk through business issues with his agent and the Chargers. Since we hadn't gotten to see too much of New York City, we asked the driver to show us around. We saw Times Square, Trump Tower, and Central Park. The kids wanted to walk around Central Park, but I wasn't interested.

"People show up missing when they go in that park," I said.

But they just laughed it off, got out of the car, and left. I went back to the hotel. I was exhausted—happy, but exhausted.

|||

LaDainian flew to California immediately after the draft, and with the help of his agent, he moved into a two-bedroom condominium in a suburb of San Diego. The move hadn't come quickly enough for him; he was so antsy to get there and get to work.

"I have to move out there, because Ricky Williams has gone out there and he may be trying to get my job!" he had joked. Ricky, of course, was a running back from San Diego who now played for the New Orleans Saints.

I stayed behind to handle the college apartment stuff and my job in real estate.

Of course, once Dainian was in San Diego, I worried about him. He didn't know a soul except for Drew. But he didn't care; he was charged with anticipation and optimism. This was it—his dream had come true. He unpacked, got settled in, and looked forward to going to training camp. His contract was still in negotiations, and he was waiting for word that everything had been settled.

But instead of "ready, set, go," he got "ready, set, *whoa*"! His agent and San Diego seemed to be having trouble reaching an agreement. Neither LaDainian nor I were sure about all the complexities or what was holding everything up. We left it all to the agent, but the wait was frustrating.

The first week LaDainian was in San Diego, he called my sister Bertha's son, André, and asked him to come live with him and be his bodyguard and assistant. Having someone from home helped. Then a month later, Torsha transferred her college credits to the University of California, San Diego, and moved out there.

Dainian called me every other day with the same news: "There's no word."

Finally in August, he called. "It's done, Mom."

"What does that mean, baby?" I asked.

Never in my life would I have thought that "It's done" meant a multimillion-dollar contract. I almost fell over when I learned what his salary would be. My knees went weak, and I had to ask him to repeat what he'd just told me. *Oh, God,* I prayed. *I never imagined You'd give him this.*

Within a matter of months, my son went from being a college kid to a multimillionaire. But as wonderful as that contract was, it came at a cost. The negotiations had taken so long that he hadn't been able to go to training camp and had to work out on his own. He missed all of the preseason except for the last game that was going to be played in Arizona.

LaVar, André, Londria, her two kids, and I hopped on a plane and were at that Arizona game. I wanted to be there the first time LaDainian stepped foot on the field as a professional football player. Even though we were in the nosebleed section, it was an electric moment for us when we saw him run out with his number 21 jersey. At least I think it was him! They wouldn't allow us to have our binoculars, so I squinted through most of the game. It was like watching someone on TV. I would soon discover that even for family members, away game seats leave a lot to be desired. They aren't the worst seats, but they are the leftovers that nobody wants.

They won that game. Ironically, that was one of only three preseason games he has played. Because he was a starter, the coach didn't like to put him in exhibition games for fear of risking an injury during preseason when the games didn't count.

LaDainian had just played his first professional game—and

we knew he was going to gain momentum. He did well, but the momentum wasn't going to last long. Not only did the contract negotiations cause him to miss his training and the preseason, but the terrorist attacks of September 11, 2001, hit, causing football to be put on the back burner for a while. So now he had to sit and wait to play a little longer.

CHAPTER 18

The Quiet Rookie

THE REGULAR SEASON had begun, and the Chargers were gearing up for their first home game. As I prepared for the trip, I was about to burst with excitement.

TCU had always given me complimentary tickets to the games. The Chargers didn't, so Dainian had to pay for them, but at least we received parking passes so we could meet him in a private parking area. I couldn't believe it!

I'm sure LaDainian was nervous about playing in the professional league—but I think I might have been more so. I wanted him to do well—and survive the game intact! He might not have walked out onto the field thinking, *The goal is to make it through this game with nothing broken, pulled, or torn*, but I sure thought it!

Instead he just kept telling me over and over, "I have a job doing what I love to do! I get to play football and get paid for it!" His words made such an impression on me. How many times had I worked a job that I hated simply because we needed to survive? Now my son got paid to do the thing he was most passionate about. God had been so good to him. God had blessed his tenacious hard work.

A few days before game day, LaDainian gave us special instructions about which gate to use. Torsha and I were going to the

game together, and we were both so excited we chattered the
entire way to the stadium. We talked about how we couldn't wait
to see him run out onto the field, how good he looked in his
uniform, and on and on. When we finally arrived, we drove up to
the gate and handed the man our passes.

He looked at them and handed them back.

"You have to go down there." He pointed toward a spot
farther from the stadium.

"What?" I said. "No, no. My son said that we were to go
through this gate."

"I don't care what your son said. You don't have passes for this
gate." His words were clipped and he waved me on, ready to deal
with the next car. Apparently, we had the pass that goes with the
car, but we needed another pass that we didn't have. I figured if
I just told the man who my son was, that would clear up everything and he would let us in.

"Look," I said, "my son is LaDainian Tomlinson, your new
running back."

"Yeah, right," he scoffed.

"No, really," Torsha chimed in, leaning across the seat
toward my window. "This is Loreane Tomlinson, LaDainian's
mother."

I was getting ready to pull out my driver's license, but he still
wasn't buying it. He sent us packing.

"I don't care who you are—you aren't getting in here. Now
move along."

I wasn't about to let his rudeness spoil this experience for us,
so we parked where he indicated and hiked halfway around the
stadium to our seats.

When we got there, I couldn't believe how great the seats were.
They were under the eaves around the fifty yard line—much better than our seats in Arizona had been. Torsha and I got settled
in the family section. Two men seated behind us began talking

about my son. I didn't try to eavesdrop, but when you hear your son's name, your ears just automatically perk up.

"Well, let's just see what this LT is all about," one said. "We'll see if he's as good as all his hype."

I knew he would be, but my concern was more for his safety. I had seen the size of these men and how hard they tackle, so I prayed that LaDainian would *survive* the first game! After all, he was playing with the big boys now.

We enjoyed the game and the electric atmosphere of professional football. I had been to only one professional game before, and that was when Dainian was around thirteen or fourteen. I thought back to that game and smiled. It had been a Dallas home game against the San Francisco 49ers. When Joe Montana, the 49ers' quarterback, came out onto the field, Dainian's mouth dropped open and stayed that way the entire game. Now I wondered if there would be kids watching my son play who would do the same.

As soon as LaDainian stepped out onto the field, we were on our feet cheering. I couldn't tell where he was looking because of his visor. In college he had always looked up to where he knew I would be sitting. But now he was in the professional league, and I figured he was concentrating on this new world he had just entered. Even though we weren't able to make eye contact, I was still so excited for him.

I thought of Mary, the mother of Jesus. The Bible says that when Jesus was born, she pondered all these things in her heart. My boy was definitely not the Messiah, but I certainly pondered that game and that day in my heart.

Thankfully, LaDainian played well, and the two men behind us agreed that they would keep him. And he stayed alive and unhurt, so I was pleased.

Later, after that first home game, I saw Coach Norv Turner and told him how rudely the man at the gate had spoken to us. I didn't think the players' families should be treated that way, though I admitted that we might not have had the pass we needed. Since Dainian was a rookie, he probably didn't know exactly what he needed to give us. I just wanted the coach to be aware of our experience in case other rookies found themselves in the same boat. He thanked me for reporting it and promised to take care of it.

At the next game, the attendants at the gate were stumbling all over themselves to help us. I hadn't asked for special treatment; I simply asked not to be talked to rudely. After all, all the players' families had made major sacrifices throughout their lives to get their boys to this place. We had a lot invested in these men, and we wanted to enjoy the game as much as the other fans did.

|||

What a first year that turned out to be! LaDainian went from relative obscurity to being in the national spotlight. He had felt a lot of it when he started getting attention his junior year in college. But there are a lot more people who follow professional teams than college teams. And the buzz wasn't just in Texas anymore; it was all over the country.

It seemed that everywhere LaDainian went, people knew him, and they wanted him to sign anything and everything. Once, a man walked up to him, turned around, pulled up his shirt, and said, "Sign me."

Every time Dainian and I were out together somewhere and a fan would approach, I was amazed. It was as if I kept forgetting that my son was a famous athlete. I was glad my first experience of listening to fans' comments at the season opener had been positive, because the comments I heard weren't always that way. It's difficult to love somebody so deeply and hear other people—who don't know your child at all except for what they see two hours every few weeks during football season—make hateful, spiteful, mean-spirited remarks about him. It cuts so deeply into my soul.

Every time I overheard those comments, I thought, *Don't these people know that every player is someone's son or husband or brother? Would they want some stranger talking about their loved one that way?*

During one game our kicker missed some of his field goals and extra points. The crowd was very unhappy. I noticed a little boy who couldn't have been more than three years old standing up and watching a field goal attempt. He was as cute as a button. The kicker missed and the crowd booed and hissed and yelled hateful remarks. And this little boy slapped his forehead and said, "Oh, Dad!" I cringe when I think of the things he heard about his father that day.

LaDainian always handles the comments well. He understands that people have a right to their opinions, and he appreciates the fans no matter what. For the most part, they've been encouraging and wonderful to him.

I remember one time when Dainian was signing an autograph after a game. The recipient looked at him while he was writing and said, "Ya'll stunk out there tonight!"

My son calmly handed the man his autograph and said, "We're working on it."

Those comments never seemed to bother him. Maybe it was because he was so caught up in the joy of his job. He just kept telling me, "They're paying me for something I *love* to do!"

|||

LaDainian was doing so well; he had no problem keeping up with and playing with the "big boys," as we called them. He made some great friends with the other teammates. And he still continued his workout habits. He spent extra time practicing drills and working out. And while he no longer carried the ball with him everywhere as he did when he was a child, he often held on to it when he was watching TV or just sitting at home. He also still insisted on his no-talking rule on the day of a game.

He also adopted some new habits. Starting on Wednesdays through game day, he ate nothing sweet. He didn't want the empty calories.

One habit in particular caused some of his fans to ask questions. They noticed that when he made a touchdown, he didn't celebrate in the end zone the way other players did. He simply walked over to the referee and handed him the ball.

People often asked me why he did this, and I would explain that his reason went all the way back to his Pop Warner days. When he was nine years old, Londria told him he should do a little dance when he scored. Then she taught him one to do. The first opportunity Dainian got, he put on a show and performed his routine.

The crowd liked it, but the referee looked down at him and said sternly, "Young man, you see that little thing you just did? You save that for the NFL."

I think my son was so embarrassed at being reprimanded by an authority figure that he never wanted to draw attention to himself again. From that point on, whenever he scored, he simply tossed the ball to the referees. By the time he made the pros, he said he didn't need to start dancing then because he was being paid to do a job. Plus, I think after all those years, he would have felt a little funny starting up with the dancing again—especially since he's so serious and shy.

Regardless, his ethics showed how serious he was about his position, and that earned Dainian his team's respect. The papers started talking about the "quiet rookie" becoming a team leader. They said that when he did talk, his teammates listened.

So many people marveled at his maturity and levelheadedness, but I just saw it as him being himself. He had always possessed an ardent sense of responsibility and maturity. Some people even call him an old soul. It might have been because he had to be the man of the house at such an early age. But he had always been a strong, mature force, and now that he was in the pros, that quality was more clear than ever. That didn't mean he was a pushover, though. He had always been tough. I knew he would fight and stand up for what's right and would take his work very seriously.

I was proud of LaDainian's first year. He started in all sixteen games, and by the end of that 2001 season, he had rushed for 1,236 yards, received for 367 yards, and scored a total of ten touchdowns. As a comparison, that same year, the man who won the Rookie of the Year Award, Anthony "A Train" Thomas of the Chicago Bears, had 1,183 yards rushing, twenty-two receptions for 178 yards, and seven touchdowns.

LaDainian had made it.

CHAPTER 19

New Roles

EVERYBODY HEARS about the huge amounts of money football players make—and spend. Even though LaDainian had signed a contract that would make him financially comfortable, he was still nervous about his future. He hired a financial adviser to help him with his money, and he told this man that he wanted to save as much as he could. Football is an uncertain vocation, and he wanted to protect himself financially. After all, we knew football players who had gotten injured early on, were taken out of the game, and were never heard from again.

LaDainian told me, "Mom, this is my first contract and it could be my last, so I want to be careful."

He had been receiving a check after every game and just thought that would continue through the off time, but that wasn't the case. The next check would come when he went back to work. The problem was that he had so heavily invested his paychecks that he hadn't left himself much to live on that summer. I wouldn't say he was broke—but he definitely looked forward to the paychecks starting up again! We wished someone had warned us about the pay system so he could have avoided this lean time. Like everything else, it was a learning experience. We both had a lot of learning to do.

|||

As he was getting used to his new position in the pros, I was trying to figure out my new role. My baby was now twenty-one,
so he didn't need me to be his guardian anymore to sign legal
documents or manage his affairs. I didn't mind that part so
much. He was managing his life out in San Diego fine without
me. But as every loving and involved mother understands, we
birth, we nurture and love, we sacrifice for our children, and
then one day they're gone, leaving only an empty room. They've
moved on with their lives. And we mothers are left to figure out
who we are and how we fit into this new relationship with our
children. It's a difficult transition.

It's one I wish I could say I handled smoothly and perfectly. I
had handled so much of his career to this point; I was his mama,
and I had felt so close to him. The transition was difficult for me,
but I did my best to stay out of LaDainian's business unless he
specifically called and asked for advice. Oh, I had my opinions!
But I practiced keeping them to myself—most of the time.

As he continued to play for the Chargers, he settled into his
new life in San Diego, making friends, growing closer to Torsha,
and getting involved in a great church. Really, he was doing just
fine. I had raised him to be a good, responsible man living his
life with integrity and honesty, and he was doing it. Every time I
saw him, I was struck again by who he had become.

My son is a man, I would think. But in my heart, I still saw him
as a kid. Not intentionally, of course, but I still had a tendency to
relate to him as if he were a child, even though he was making
his own decisions. I felt myself trying to walk an invisible line
between being his mother and being his adviser.

I was so proud of the choices he was making and the fact
that he was becoming known for good things. Part of me
wanted to take the credit—you know, "Train up a child in the

way he should go, and when he is old he will not depart from it" (Proverbs 22:6, NKJV). But the truth was that I trained him and God did the rest. He took hold of my boy and molded him into a beautiful, mature human being. I thank Him every day of my life for that.

I remained in Fort Worth, and while this separation was painful at the time, it was crucial. Since his Pop Warner days, it had been necessary for me to be involved in LaDainian's football activities. Back then I was mostly a fan, chauffeur, and confidant. When he reached TCU, I became a publicist, business manager, and personal assistant.

By the time he reached the pros, he had another support group in place. There was a professional agent, a business manager, and a girlfriend who would soon become his wife. Thousands of miles separated us, and it wasn't necessary for me to be as involved as I had been in the past. Even so, our close relationship transcended the miles, and some people began to question it. Did he still depend on me too much?

When a boy has business questions and goes to his father, no one thinks too much about it. But when that same young man asks his *mother*, he can be labeled a "mama's boy." As many single mothers know, there are many times when we have to be a mother and a father to a child. I was LaDainian's first financial adviser, and while I might not have a college degree in this field, I did have the hands-on experience that told me how to take a little and make a lot.

And if there was one thing that LaDainian knew, it was that I had his best interests at heart and wouldn't steer him wrong. We were both trying to make sense out of this new world of professional football, and we still had a strong business relationship. In order for him to stay focused on the game, he often told people to call me for the information they needed. But that was all about to change.

|||

LaDainian had settled well into his career. And in the midst of all the football stuff, he was moving forward in his relationship with Torsha. She had finished college, and on March 21, 2003, they were married. And he stopped sleeping with that football, thank God!

I approved of Torsha. She was—and is still—perfect for my son. She complements him well. While he's fairly shy and reserved, Torsha knows no stranger! She can make you feel as if she has known you forever, and she just puts people at ease.

She can walk around chatting with everybody. LaDainian will say to me, "Mom, look at Torsha. She doesn't even know those people." But he'll smile while he says it. He loves how comfortable and at ease she makes everybody feel. He can become too serious, and she lightens him up. She's just a wonderfully well-rounded individual who dearly loves my son and takes good care of him.

When I watched LaDainian and Torsha interact, I was always impressed by their relationship. They had a very mature love. They both had their strong beliefs and characters and individuality, and God merged them together well to make them a true couple.

There was one thing about LaDainian, though, that Torsha really struggled to get used to: his no-talking-on-game-day rule. If Torsha was anything, she was a talker. So I knew it was difficult for her.

Sometimes I would ask her, "Torsha, how is he doing?"

"He's just hardheaded, Mom. He's hardheaded."

Things were going well in their marriage, and I enjoyed having a daughter-in-law who loved God and my son. But I was still trying to figure out my role as a mother of an adult, married son. I knew they had to make their own path and decisions—even though I might not agree. I had to learn to keep my opinions to myself!

Whenever someone becomes famous, the rumor mills go into overdrive, especially if romance is involved. And that's exactly what happened when LaDainian and Torsha married.

Try as you may, gossip is hard to escape. Everywhere you go tongues are wagging. In the break room at work, outside the church doors, and at parties, there is always a group of people leaning in a little closer to hear the dirt dished. So it was with Torsha and LaDainian's marriage. I began to hear things from a family friend. They weren't good things.

But I had always told the kids to be careful who they brought home and that marriage was a serious step. Dainian was smart; he knew how to surround himself with good people. I knew that all I could do was trust my son. He had a good head on his shoulders and was deeply in love with Torsha, and I knew that she treated him well and seemed to love him deeply. That's all I really needed to know.

As time passed, I forgot the rumors, but the talebearer didn't. She began to tell Torsha bits of made-up gossip about me. Several months later she made a trip out to San Diego to visit my son and daughter-in-law. While she was there taking advantage of their generosity, she told them that I was casting aspersions upon my new daughter-in-law's integrity.

Both Dainian and Torsha were hurt and angered, and rightfully so. And I felt betrayed because someone had twisted a casual conversation, giving it a different, almost sinister connotation. I couldn't understand why she chose to manipulate the situation like this. What was her gain, other than to destroy my family?

By the time the visit was over, this woman had done terrible damage to my relationship with my son and daughter-in-law. I was blindsided when LaDainian called and asked me about it. I couldn't believe he was asking me about this, and I grew defensive.

I paid dearly for this person's stories. My family was torn

apart, and although we continued to talk over the phone, we spent no holidays together, and I attended none of his games that year. The only thing I remember about those months is the tears.

Often I would pull out and reread the letter he wrote me when he was in high school. *If he trusted me then and knew my character, if he understood how much I loved him then, why is he questioning me now?* I wondered. *Why is he taking this woman's word over mine?* I could understand Torsha questioning my motives—she hadn't known me as long and didn't have the history LaDainian and I shared. But my son knew me; he had history with me that had been consistent throughout his entire life.

As I daily prayed over the situation, the Lord reminded me that the truth would win out, that I just needed to be patient. But nothing seemed to change. Until the next year when my mother died.

Even at our lowest point, when we wonder if God has forgotten about us, He is still working. He is always doing something. He used my mother's death to remind us that life is too short for the foolishness of being estranged from family. He was really working on my heart during this time, and it turns out, He was working on all of us.

LaDainian called to ask how I was doing after my mother's death. I became angry. I said, "I lost my mom. I've been going over in my mind what kind of time I could have spent with her that I didn't. How many times I could have told her that I loved her and I didn't. Now I can't. Once I'm gone I don't want you ever to go through that. There should *never* be a time that you do not know how much I love you, and love never hurt anybody. We should do everything we can to show the people we love how much we love and appreciate them. Because, baby, once they're gone, they're gone. You can't get them back.

"We don't have a lot of time together. We never know when

this time will be our last. Dainian, we love each other with everything we have. There is nothing you could do that would make me stop loving you. And I would never stop trusting you."

We both began to cry.

"LaDainian, we are from a family who love one another. We know the Lord. He expects more from us. I'm sorry for my part in this, and I want us to be a family again."

For the first time since our estrangement, it felt like God was working to heal our family.

Dainian and Torsha came to Marlin several days before my mother's funeral. That was the first time I had seen them in almost a year. It felt wonderful, as if everything was okay. We talked and laughed together, and there was no trace of any resentment or problem.

At the funeral, Torsha walked straight over to me, put her arms around me, and whispered, "Mom, I love you." I knew she meant it.

I held on to her and said, "And I love you." And I meant it.

Something melted in me. I had done a lot of searching within myself over the previous year. And I realized that some of the tension was the result of new roles and expectations in our family that were tough to figure out.

I thought back to my own marriage and my relationship with my mother-in-law. Tee and his mom had a special relationship, and sometimes it felt threatening to me. She was his mom; she'd changed his diapers and taken care of him when he was a baby. She had history with him that I didn't share. There were times when I felt Tee was giving his mom some of what should have been mine.

I felt God whispering to me, *You have to step back. Let Dainian find himself, let Torsha find herself, and let them make their way in their marriage. You're not a threat to her, and she's not a threat to you.*

We women can try to compete when a man we love is

involved. I didn't want to be that kind of person. My son deserved better.

I looked again at this lovely young lady my son had married. *I'm going to be the best mother-in-law I can be,* I determined.

Out of those ashes I learned some valuable lessons. Love your family for who they are; know them and trust them. Meet them where they are. They can't be who they are not. Life is too short to hurt people with careless remarks. It just isn't worth the pain.

Our relationship grew stronger after that. I looked forward to returning to Dainian's home games. Torsha and I always went together, so I was glad we would be able to spend time together, just the two of us, watching the man we both loved so much.

Torsha reminds me a lot of myself. She has even told me that several times Dainian has told her the same thing.

He'll say, "Girl, you're not my mama."

"I know I'm not your mama. Your mama's back in Texas. But you're always *telling* me I remind you of your mama!" she shoots back at him.

Hearing those stories makes me laugh.

Whenever I traveled to San Diego for the home games, I always stayed with them, and it was the most wonderful time. It was like being in a different world, because they treated me like royalty. I would fly in the day before the game, and Torsha and I would spend that first evening just chatting. Sometimes Dainian was there watching games on TV, or sometimes he was working out or getting his muscles rubbed down. Either way, I treasured that Torsha-and-me time.

Believe it or not, I didn't get to spend too much time with Dainian when I was there because he was in and out so much. So on Sunday mornings, usually the day of the game, I would go in and sit with him. Of course, he wouldn't talk, so I just held his hand and sat, relishing the time in his presence. He usually had four TVs going, watching the competition and their plays. Staying focused for the job he had to do. And I knew we were good. Just my son and me and football.

||

Our joy completely returned when LaDainian and Torsha announced they were having a baby in 2005. He had always been focused on his career, but he also had a more important goal: to have a family. Now it seemed this final piece of the puzzle was falling into place.

"Do you know what it's going to be?" I asked excitedly.

"No. We decided not to learn the sex of the baby. We want it to be a surprise."

But when Torsha had a sonogram, LaDainian accidentally found out they were having a girl. He asked her again and again if she wanted to know.

"No," she repeatedly told him.

Unfortunately, Dainian has never been good with surprises. Finally, one night he could stand it no longer and blurted out, "Torsha, we're having a girl—our little princess."

Our family was elated. I was going to be a grandma again! Not only were Dainian and Torsha expecting, but LaVar and his wife, Nikki, were too. Within a few months of each other, both of my boys would become fathers for the first time.

But about seven months into Torsha's pregnancy, I received a call. It was LaDainian. I was a little surprised to hear from him because they were on vacation.

When I answered, all he said was, "Mom."

My son is a man of few words, but the following silence spoke volumes. Fear filled my body and my throat constricted. I knew that something was terribly wrong.

"What is it, Dainian?" I asked.

There was still no reply. Tears filled my eyes. *What could it be?* My mind raced through all the possibilities. "Son, what's wrong?"

After another pause he spoke very softly. "We lost the baby. Makiah."

Shocked and stunned, all I could manage was, "What?"

"Torsha hadn't been feeling the baby moving, so we went to the hospital. They told us that the baby died."

"Oh, Dainian," I cried. "I'm so, so sorry, baby. Should I come?"

"No, Mom, we're just going to take care of everything down here, and then we're going to leave town for a while."

Over the years I have been told that I tend to overstep my boundaries. But I knew when my son said that, he meant I shouldn't come. This was just between LaDainian and Torsha. The only thing I knew to do was to respect their privacy and grieve alone. Heartbreaking doesn't begin to describe the pain we all went through. LaDainian had always said he wanted to be the best son, husband, and father he could be. He was already the best son and husband. And I knew that he was also the best father for this precious baby, even though he would never hold her in his arms and rock her to sleep or bounce her in the air and listen to her laugh and call him "Daddy."

There are times today when I look at LaVar's oldest daughter and think that she should have a cousin the same age, and it breaks my heart all over again.

LaDainian has often said, "You really think you're in control of your life, and then something comes along and slaps you in the face. It makes you realize you're not in control." Losing Makiah made him look at things in a different light, realizing that nobody is invincible. Everybody goes through difficult situations in their lives. The key is how we handle those situations.

"God definitely used LaDainian for me," Torsha told me. "I was a wreck. LaDainian is my rock. He sacrificed his own need to

grieve, pushed it to the back, to stand up and be there for me."
For us all.

|||

LaDainian tucked the pain of his loss deep inside himself. He
had to be strong for those of us who couldn't be. But he also
threw himself into his work even more.

It was as if every time he went onto the field, even if it was
just for a couple of hours, he was once again able to enjoy himself like he had when he was a kid. Maybe that was his way of
dealing with the loss.

But he felt such a responsibility to his team that he took
every loss personally. Even though he was having a great year
(that season he rushed for 1,462 yards and received for 370
yards, for a total of 1,832 yards, and made twenty touchdowns),
he wouldn't let up on himself.

Even when the Chargers won, he would say, "Mom, I could
have done better."

I tried to take his comments in stride, knowing he was a
perfectionist and that he felt the game so deeply. But I was also
concerned that he was holding too much inside.

The one highlight of that year was that his team was getting
closer and closer to the Super Bowl. The Chargers had gone to
the play-offs every year after his rookie season. The pull for that
Super Bowl ring was so powerful, LaDainian said he could feel
it on his finger. But it always seemed just out of reach.

CHAPTER 20

Giving Back

I CONTINUED to be overwhelmed by how well LaDainian settled into the NFL and slammed record after record. Two years after he made it to the pros, we returned to our stomping grounds in Waco for a ceremony where University High School retired his jersey. He was so touched by that gesture.

In 2005, he established himself as a "triple threat" when he rushed for eighteen touchdowns, received two touchdowns, and threw for four. Dainian was tearing up the field. It was then that former Charger fullback Lorenzo Neal gave him the nickname "Superman without the cape."

And in 2006, he rushed for 1,815 yards and received fifty-six passes for 508 yards, for a total of 2,323 yards and thirty-one touchdowns, which was a record for the most touchdowns in a single season. He helped take his team to a league best 14–2 season and postseason play.

LaDainian continued to work just as hard keeping his body and mind in top shape. He had an exercise regimen that was so top secret even I didn't know all of it. Part of it included running a hill that he'd built in his backyard for conditioning. This was one of the things his childhood idol, Walter Payton, did to stay in top condition.

We still stayed connected throughout the games. No longer did he pick up tickets for us for the home games. He simply worked it into his contract so that we were able to sit in our own box—we had some of the best seats in the house! But we no longer sat with the other family members and fans, and I, for one, missed that—even though it was nice that Dainian knew exactly where we were seated.

Whenever he made a great play, he would point a finger into the air. He told us he did that to give thanks to God but also to connect with us. Even on the field, he was always thinking about his family. Sitting so far away from him, I could still feel that strong connection, and my chest filled with pride and love every time I saw him.

|||

During his time in Texas and San Diego, LaDainian was becoming more and more of a celebrity. But he was still able to keep a fairly low profile—until 2006.

I think God gives us ordinary days in order to center us and prepare us for the unexpected. The day began like a hundred others. When the phone rang around noon, I was not surprised to hear Dainian's voice. He was on his first break during football practice.

"Hey Mom, how are you doing?" he asked.

"Good," I said. "How are you?"

"Fine," he said, and then continued with small talk. Finally, he casually said, "Did you hear I won MVP?"

"Oh, Dainian!" I exclaimed. "I hadn't heard! That's wonderful. I am so proud of you!"

We all felt so honored. That year he was awarded the National Football League's 2006 Most Valuable Player Award for his performance on the field and the NFL's 2006 Man of the Year for his charity work.

LaDainian became only the second player to win both awards in the same season. Walter Payton, for whom the Man of the Year award is named, was the first.

Dainian really took his talents seriously. He had always felt that if he was going to play the game, he wanted to be the best, to leave a mark on the game. If the record was there, it could be broken. But he didn't play just to break the record. He would say, "Do I set my mind to just go on the field and break the record? No. But I play with my whole mind, body, and soul. So if there's a record I break, that's fine."

He still compared his goals to what his role models Emmitt Smith and Walter Payton had done.

"Walter Payton was an awesome person," Dainian said. "I want to be mentioned as a Walter Payton–type person." He even named his white pit bull after Payton: Sweetness—Payton's nickname.

LaDainian's football career has afforded him the opportunity to meet people like Tiger Woods, Will Smith, Magic Johnson, and Michael Jordan. And he continued to have unusually close rela- tionships with other players who kept him grounded in his faith, particularly Drew Brees (who would go on to become the quar- terback for the New Orleans Saints).

Dainian had already been doing some endorsements, but with the MVP honor, his list of product endorsements grew. He worked with such companies as Nike, AT&T, HomeTurf, Fisher-Price, Canon, ESPN Radio, Vizio electronics, Vitaminwater, Oggi's Pizza, and Campbell's soup.

Torsha and Dainian enjoyed sharing the perks of some of his endorsements as well. We never knew when we would receive some surprise in the mail, courtesy of one of his sponsors. He made sure that his nieces and nephews had his shoes—he had his own line of LT Nikes—for back-to-school time. One Christmas they sent LaVar's daughters matching pink outfits with "Tomlinson 21" on them, complete with pink caps and Nike shoes.

The endorsement that really surprised me, however, was the one that included me. I was at home when I received a call from a Campbell's representative asking me to be in a Chunky Soup commercial with Dainian. I relished the idea of spending some time with him and making a little money on the side.

My role was easy: I simply had to hang out a window, shout, "LaDainian," and motion for him to come in and eat. We made the commercial with other players and their moms, and I had fun getting to know everybody. The guys had to play football in the mud and cold for days. If the ground got a little too dry, the production assistants would water it and make it rain or snow until it was soupy again. No pun intended.

It took hours of work just to create a sixty-second spot! I felt so honored that Campbell's included me in their commercial. The moms with their guys were a lot of fun. We all pulled for one another's sons during the games and kept track of how everybody was doing. But the best part of the commercial work was that it gave me something I always long for: time with my son. His "off-season" was so filled with his charity work, business commitments, and intense physical training, it was difficult to get a lot of time with him. Thankfully, we continued to talk on the phone frequently.

For all the accolades, awards, endorsements, and broken records, though, I never saw anything but humility and graciousness in LaDainian. When I saw his strong faith and the way he lived his life, I just felt overwhelmingly proud. Torsha called him "maddeningly nonchalant," and it's true, he did begin to grow more comfortable in the spotlight. But he still squirmed if someone called him famous. I think this is partly because as passionate as he was about football, it wasn't his only goal in life. Football was what he did for a living, but it didn't define him.

He even put his foot down with Torsha when she suggested decorating their game room in their home by wrapping the custom bar and trophy case in pigskin. He told her, "I don't want pigskins in my house." He didn't want anybody to think that his whole life was just about football. And although he had some memorabilia from other players, he never liked to display his own items. He thought it made him seem conceited.

LaDainian's priorities remained the same: his faith in God, his family, and then football. "Hopefully everything will go hand in hand," he told one reporter. "Hopefully I can become stronger with God and be able to touch people's lives that way. Hopefully I'll have a big family and hopefully I'll get a Super Bowl ring."[1]

|||

If I was proud of LaDainian's accomplishments in football, it was nothing compared to the pleasure I felt watching the strength of his character and his accomplishments off the field.

As Dainian and Torsha struggled with their grief over losing Makiah, they reached out to their community in California and in Texas and helped make others' lives better by starting the Tomlinson Touching Lives Foundation. LaDainian wanted to recreate the magic he felt as a youth in the Jay Novacek/Emmitt Smith camp. He wanted to inspire kids the way he had been inspired. He never forgot when Emmitt Smith handed the ball to him. That one moment of inspiration changed his life.

The foundation really started when he did his first camp back at his high school in Waco. He looked at those kids' faces and how excited they were to be around a football player from their neighborhood who had made it. From there he decided to include summer camps in San Diego and Fort Worth.

Eventually, the foundation would grow to include many different events each year, from the 21 Club to "School is

Cool" to youth football camps, a golf tournament, complete
Thanksgiving dinners to families, fishing trips for kids, and a
Christmas program in which more than 1,500 holiday gifts
would be distributed to the patients at San Diego's children's
hospital and health center.

As much as the football camp inspired him, I think the
church youth camp he'd attended also played a huge role in
LaDainian's wanting to reach out and give back to people in
need. I am a firm believer in the Word of God. And it says the
footsteps of a righteous man are ordered by God. God started
ordering Dainian's footsteps way back then for what he would
need to do in the future.

LaDainian knew that while football is wonderful, what's truly
important in life is helping people, giving back some of the bless-
ings we have received. I was so proud that Dainian understood
that. Of course, I was proud of him when he received the 2006
Man of the Year award for his outreach and work in different
communities. But the awards really mean nothing; it's what is
in the heart that will last for eternity.

CHAPTER 21

The Super Bowl That Almost Was

LADAINIAN HAD A GREAT YEAR professionally in 2006. But personally he was struggling. He was still grieving the loss of his little princess, Makiah, when my sister Bertha died. Bertha was my best friend and his favorite aunt. We both loved her dearly. She had rheumatoid arthritis and was forced to use a walker, but other than that she was healthy, so we were shocked in May when she experienced either a massive heart attack or an aneurysm and dropped dead, leaving our family reeling from the loss. She went so quickly, we never had the chance to say good-bye.

What made our grief even more intense was the fact that we were planning a family reunion, and she was heading it up. Once again, we were reminded that we never know how long we'll have with somebody we love. Our time with her was cut too short. Dainian and I tried to comfort each other and Bertha's son André, who had become Dainian's personal assistant during his rookie year.

We had barely begun to get used to the idea that Bertha was gone, when seven months later, another tragedy hit.

On February 23, 2007, Tee and his son Ronald were driving from Tomlinson Hill back to Ron's house in Waco. Ronald's truck was old and run down; he used it to get around the farm and feed the animals.

As they traveled down the back roads toward Waco, a tire blew and the truck swerved out of control on the gravel road and flipped over. Tee was thrown from the truck and died instantly. Ronald slammed through the windshield.

Ronald was rushed by ambulance to Waco's Hillcrest Baptist Medical Center, but he died later that day.

A woman who knew Tee from Tomlinson Hill called me a few hours after the accident.

"Loreane, have you heard about Tee?"

"What about him?" I asked.

She paused for a moment. I sensed her discomfort and felt my stomach tighten.

"He was killed in an accident."

My knees went weak.

"Oh, my Lord, no!" was all I could say.

"I'm so sorry," she said over and over.

When I was finally able to catch my breath, I thanked her for calling. Immediately, I called some of Tee's relatives to find out what had happened. As soon as I discovered the news was all true, I called my kids. But LaDainian and Torsha were on a plane headed to Tennessee for business.

I kept calling and texting them, and finally after several hours, Torsha called.

"What's going on?" she asked. "We have all these calls and texts."

"Sweetheart, I have some bad news," I told her, a lump forming in my throat. "LaDainian's father has been killed in an accident."

"Oh, no," Torsha said, choking up.

"You're going to need to put your arms around him, hug him, and tell him. But keep me on the phone, because his brother

Ron was in the truck too, and he's in the hospital. It doesn't look good for him."

She said, "Okay," then I heard her muffled voice as she told him.

LaDainian yelled, "Oh, my God, *no!*" And then he began to sob in a manner that I had heard only once before—the day I told him I knew he had been drinking.

I've never felt so helpless in my life. I was miles away with no ability to comfort him. All I could offer was more bad news.

"Baby, I'm so sorry," I said when he finally got on the phone. "I'm so, so sorry."

"Mom," he cried. His voice caught in his throat, and all he could do was whimper.

How can I tell him about his brother, Lord? I prayed. I didn't want to have to tell him more bad news. But I knew I had to.

"He was with Ron," I began. "They were driving from Tomlinson Hill back to Waco to Ron's house when the truck's tire blew. Your dad died instantly, but baby, Ron is in the hospital. They don't know if he's going to make it."

How much more could we take? My mother, Makiah, my sister Bertha, and now Tee. And by three o'clock that afternoon, we lost Ron.

"We're on our way," Dainian said once he was able to speak again.

He and Torsha flew home to California immediately to handle a few affairs, and then they flew to Fort Worth so we could drive to Marlin together.

At a time when we should have been able to mourn privately, peacefully, and quietly, Dainian instead had to deal with family conflict and media intrusions. My cousin, the sheriff of Marlin, had done an excellent job controlling the crowds at my mom's and sister's services. Even though those two services hadn't made the news, swarms of people from Marlin and the surrounding area had shown up to get LaDainian's photo and autograph. Even at the burial, people were trying to get him to sign something.

Tee's death, though, was different. Reports of the accident and death were splattered all over the national news. We knew that the situation could quickly spiral out of control, so we tried to keep the whole thing as understated and respectful as possible. We were going to need my cousin to keep control of the funeral.

Dainian told the funeral director to spare no expense but explained that we wanted to have the service in Marlin so Tee's friends, most of whom were elderly, could make it to the church more easily. But one of Tee's relatives wanted a double service held in Waco, where Ron had lived, and was pushing for one of the largest, most elaborate churches there.

We didn't want the funeral there, though. In Marlin my cousin could manage the situation and curtail the media and everybody else. If we went to Waco, we would be totally on our own. And that just about ensured it would be a circus.

Rather than have our family fight over the funeral, LaDainian said, "We are not going to keep my daddy from being buried, so go ahead and have the service in Waco. But we will not attend. We will have our own funeral here in Marlin."

We would have the first service in Marlin for Tee and Ron, and then they could move the caskets to Waco and hold a second service there. The bodies would then be transported back to the cemetery outside of Marlin. We thought that would take care of it. But that didn't seem to make anyone happy either. Florists were prevented from delivering flowers to the funeral home in Marlin because a relative wanted all the flowers and sympathy cards in Waco only.

Even though Dainian paid for his father's funeral—the limousines, guest books, and all the other incidentals—we never received any of the sympathy cards people sent and we weren't even allowed to get the guest book. Even the tri-fold programs we ordered weren't delivered to us but remained in Waco with the other relatives. Instead, the funeral director photocopied single sheets of a quickly typed-out program and passed those out for us to use. (After the funeral, when LaDainian went to finish paying the expenses, the director handed him the box of tri-fold programs we had originally ordered. The Waco attenders got to use them, but we didn't. When I learned about that, I thought, *May the Lord have mercy on that man for the grief and sorrow he caused our family.*)

Later, when LaDainian went on national television to thank the country for all the support, he explained that we hadn't been able to acknowledge their expressions of sympathy because we were never given the cards from the flowers or the guest book.

After we had our service, we gathered with friends and relatives for a meal and fellowship. We didn't even attend the burial because LaDainian's celebrity status would have drawn too many onlookers, reporters, and autograph seekers. It is one of the terrible downsides to his fame. He couldn't even grieve properly or normally for his father.

Afterward, we did feel cheated that we weren't allowed to grieve and see Tee and Ronald put in their final resting places. It bothered me to think that my children couldn't have that closure. But we tried not to dwell on that. The service we had was what Tee would have wanted. Tee was a simple man with simple tastes. He was surrounded by his family and friends. A few simple flower arrangements would have been more than enough to please him. Tee was buried in a secluded cemetery not far from Tomlinson Hill, the place he loved, his home. Dainian waited a few months for the media frenzy to die down before visiting the grave site so that he could have some privacy.

For months after Tee's death, LaDainian mourned. He questioned time and again if there wasn't one more thing he could have said or done to help his father. For all the years that Dainian was in San Diego, he had begged his father to move out there with him. But Tee wouldn't do it—he wanted to remain on the Hill. Dainian did everything he could to encourage Tee to get help and get healthy. But Tee was content to remain on the Hill the way he was.

Tee and LaDainian had reconnected during his senior year at TCU. His dad had also attended a couple of the pro games and was immensely proud of his son. I think LaDainian's drive for the Super Bowl was partly fueled by his longing to please his dad. But LaDainian's attempts to help his father with his addiction had been futile.

LaDainian had offered his dad everything imaginable, from medical help to a nicer home to a place in his San Diego home. Dainian would have given him anything he wanted or needed. But Tee always refused. LaDainian had never given up on him though. He had always felt that if he could get Tee out to San Diego, his life would be so much better.

But I understood something LaDainian didn't: being on Tomlinson Hill made Tee happy. In Tee's mind, the memories of the past were strong and present. Mother Julie was still there baking cookies, brothers were going fishing, and young sons and daughters were playing. The spirits of everyone who had passed through his life were still there. And as the caretaker of those memories, he felt he needed to stay. Living in a mansion didn't appeal to him. Everything he needed was right there on Tomlinson Hill.

Even so, the frustration of the situation seldom left LaDainian's mind. Money couldn't buy everything; if it could, his father would be well and living in comfort surrounded by his loved ones. What made it worse was that every now and then a reporter would track Tee down, write a story about the "deplorable" conditions in which Tee lived—according to the reporter's view—and there would be a public outcry that the San Diego

Chargers' LaDainian Tomlinson was letting his father live in a small, run-down home.

The problem was that the reporter typically judged the conditions based on big-city living. The truth was that it was a four-bedroom, two-bath house that sat on a quarter of an acre. By country standards, it wasn't all that bad! Maybe it was the tin roof that Tee liked, but that the reporter misunderstood. All the same, these accusations sliced through Dainian's heart and ours because we all knew the countless attempts Dainian had made to relocate him. Now, it was over.

|||

A short time after the funeral, LaVar and his family and I drove out to San Diego to be with LaDainian and Torsha.

While we were there, LaDainian came to me and asked, "Mom, was Dad a good man?"

"Of course he was," I said. "Look at you; you are a good and decent man. You are a part of both of us. Your dad was a good, decent, kindhearted man too. I don't think that either of us could have loved him if he wasn't."

I began to tell him some of the things his father had gone through. I tried to reassure Dainian that his father was a believer. Perhaps his faith hadn't been as strong as ours, but he definitely believed in God. I could still picture him reading from his big family King James Bible.

"We never know what's in a man's heart or how God deals with him," I explained. "Your dad would give a hungry man his last dollar. He would feed him. He would look for ways to bless and help people. That's who he was. Everybody deals with issues, baby, and there are some things that are going to keep you on your knees. Well, your father stumbled on something that was bigger than he was, and he never quite conquered it."

I thought about it for a moment. I don't think Tee believed that he *could* overcome his addiction. That's why he didn't. Being in constant pain causes you to focus on the pain itself, not on the healing. But God can do anything, and He's certainly stronger than those prescription drugs. I just wish Tee had understood that.

I smiled at my son. "What do you think?"

"Yeah, he loved us and we loved him," he replied. "But now he's gone. I just wish we'd had more time together before he died."

I agreed—it was important to me to express to him how precious time is with the people we love. The ones we have today may not be with us tomorrow. Too often we take that time for granted.

Bertha's, Ronald's, and Tee's deaths served as reminders that we must cherish the here and now. Life is so frail.

"Never pass up a chance to tell the ones you love that you love them," I told him. "Because you may never get that chance again."

We talked about the last time they were together and how joyful that time had been. In a rare occurrence, all three kids, Londria, LaVar, and LaDainian, had gotten together to take Tee to dinner. They talked and laughed and took photos. That spontaneous family reunion was the last time LaDainian saw his father.

I looked at my handsome son and thought back to when Tee and I divorced. I remembered Dainian asking me over and over, "When's Daddy coming home, Mama?" Now as I looked at the sadness in my grown son's eyes, I realized that he had never stopped asking himself that question. LaDainian's dream of having his father by his side, sharing his career and the advantages it brought with it, wasn't going to happen.

|||

Tragedy wasn't through with LaDainian, though. That fall, just as the 2007 season rolled around, wildfires began burning throughout San Diego County and the surrounding areas. California was fighting some of the worst wildfires in their history, and those fires were headed right toward LaDainian and Torsha's home.

This wasn't the first time they had been faced with the fire furies. Three years earlier they had evacuated another home. Back then LaDainian had called and said, "Mom, it looks like the fire is right in our backyard, but it's not. It's a couple of miles away."

"Son, don't try to be a hero," I scolded. "Evacuate. You can buy another house, but you need to protect Torsha and yourself."

Fortunately, that fire had turned and their house was saved. This time, however, the fires were taking direct aim at their neighborhood in Poway, a suburb of San Diego. The reports were all over the news, and people were frantically calling me to see if the kids were okay.

I was relieved when LaDainian called and said that they had left their home and were staying at a hotel with their three dogs. The only thing we could do was wait to see the fate of their beautiful home. Wanting to stay busy and keep their minds off their home situation, LaDainian traveled with the rest of the team to Arizona for football practice while Torsha went to their home in Austin, Texas, to await word.

Finally, after several days, the officials gave the okay for people to return to their neighborhood. Former Atlanta Braves baseball player David Justice, whose house was around the corner from Dainian and Torsha's, let my son know that the Tomlinson home had been saved. But poor David had lost everything, even all his treasured sports memorabilia. I was impressed and grateful that he had taken the time to lift LaDainian's burden when he was carrying such a heavy one himself.

While their house hadn't been burned, it did have smoke damage. And they lost all the fish in their huge aquarium because the electricity had gone out, causing the oxygen regulator to stop. They had been fortunate that their loss was minimal. And their hearts went out to those who had lost everything.

LaDainian purchased and arranged to pass out three hundred flat-screen TVs to the victims of the fire. It was his way of trying to comfort those who had lost so much.

The fires were under control enough for San Diego to return to their stadium to play. And with smoke still thick in the air, the Chargers got back to business.

I flew out to do an interview with LaDainian shortly after that. The area looked like the valley of death. Even though their house had been spared, their neighborhood looked like a disaster area. There wasn't anything green; everything was charred. The smell of smoke hung heavy in the air, making it difficult to breathe.

Even though parts of California were a disaster area, the Chargers plowed ahead with their season. I worried about my son.With his father's death earlier in the year and then with so much suffering in his state, I didn't know if he would be able to focus under the burden.

But in the 2007 season, although he had faced hard times and was playing with a heavy heart, he managed to rush for 1,474 yards and received for 475 yards for a total of 1,949 yards and eighteen touchdowns.

Watching Dainian play so well was the bright spot in our lives. We were all getting excited at the thought this might be the year that they would go all the way to the Super Bowl. My poor son—after all he'd been through, I desperately wanted a Super Bowl win for him to bring some light and joy to an otherwise dark year.

It wasn't just football, I knew, that brought him comfort. I saw his faith draw him closer to God as he spent more and more time in prayer and connecting with other believers, especially the team's chaplain, Pastor Shawn. God was granting him strength. But it was mental, not necessarily physical.

During the divisional round game, in which San Diego defeated the Colts in one of the most exciting games I've seen,

LaDainian injured his knee. It happened late in the game. He went into the end zone and somebody fell on his ankle. The pressure of it twisted his leg.

LaDainian's legs are his livelihood, so we were all concerned about the extent of the injury and what it would mean, not only for his ability to play, but also for his quality of life. While the family waited for word about his injury, we prayed for the best but prepared for the worst.

Always a man of great responsibility and concern for his family, he tried to keep me from worrying and said very little. So all I could do was pray. *God, I don't know his injury. But You do. And You know how to heal and mend it.*

The next game for the Chargers was the AFC Championship Game against the Patriots—one game away from the Super Bowl. Everybody was speculating about whether or not LaDainian would be able to play.

Whenever I asked about his leg, he would barely discuss it, merely saying, "Everything's going to be fine. I don't want you to worry."

While others were asking this same question, LaDainian was preparing to play. He didn't care about the pain. My son had played through pain his whole life. He had played through groin injuries and even taken the field with broken ribs. Even so, could that knee take the abuse of a game? Would it hold up?

This was his dream game. He wanted to help lead his team into the Super Bowl. This was as close as the Chargers had ever gotten, and he wanted to be there.

After so many years of following him around to many of his games, I had started to stay home for the away games. And since this game was to take place in Boston—and in the freezing cold, which I hate—I opted to remain home and watch from the comfort and warmth of my living room.

LaDainian didn't last long on the field. His limp was pronounced, and as he headed to the sidelines, my heart sank. He tried to go back in, but he just couldn't make his body do what he wanted it to. As he walked off the field again, I knew his injury was more serious than he had been letting on. Nothing could have taken him out of this game if he had even one ounce of strength left in him.

Although he had been through many devastating experiences in a short time, he had pushed all those feelings deep down inside in order to play the game to the best of his ability. But his body just wouldn't allow him to continue. It was as if everything that had happened in the past year urfaced in the pain of his injury, and it was too much for him. Dainian took the game so seriously, he often cried when he couldn't lead the team to victory. I truly believed that behind his visor, which remained steadfastly in place, he was crying.

As I sat in my living room, I was crying too. My mind started to hear his voice: *When's Daddy coming home, Mama? . . . Mom, we lost the baby. . . . The fire is in our neighborhood— we're evacuating. . . . Was my daddy a good man? . . . I wish we'd had more time together.*

Tears rolled down my face as the camera kept focusing on my son. I never saw him move. By the end of that game our team looked like the walking wounded. The loss was a bitter disappointment. And in my mind I heard my son's voice saying, "It's okay, Mom. I'll just work harder next time."

After the game, he called me before they boarded the plane to return to San Diego. I always try to text him after the games. I'll usually write, "Good game. Call me. Love you." But this time he called before I could text him.

"Hey, Mom, what's going on?" he said. I could tell from his tone that his heart was broken.

"I'm so sorry it was such a hard game," I told him. "But we'll get them next time around."

"Yeah."

"Are you okay?"

"Yeah," he said, obviously trying to reassure me. "I just need to get some treatment, and I'll be fine."

I thanked God that *was* their last game, because I don't think he would have been fine. I don't think he would have been able to play if they *had* gotten to the Super Bowl. We didn't know it at the time, but it would take several months of rehabilitation and therapy before Dainian would begin to feel better.

Right after the game, some of the media jumped on Dainian with both feet. It seemed as if everyone had turned against him and was criticizing him either for not playing or for not being a cheerleader on the sidelines. I couldn't believe it. I knew that he had actually been cheering on his teammates, encouraging them. The cameras had only caught when he was being silent. And Dainian had never missed a game due to an injury. *Do they honestly think he would choose the biggest game of his life to start taking it easy?* I thought angrily. But what hurt me the most was the reaction of some of his fans.

Some of them complained because the quarterback, Philip Rivers, had also injured his knees yet he had continued to play. That comparison bothered me, because Philip uses his *arms*; he doesn't have to use his legs like Dainian. Dainian's *entire job* on the field depends exclusively on his legs.

I made the mistake of getting online one day, and my eye caught one of the sports blogs. So much cruelty and hatred was spewed across the screen that I had to look away. This was one of the lowest points I had hit since LaDainian started playing football when he was nine years old. I didn't understand. *What was his crime?* I thought. *That he realized he was too injured to play?* The boy loves playing football; why would he willingly walk off the field and *not* play in such an important game?

I wanted to type my own response! I wanted to write, "Stop it! It's a *game*. He has given everything he has! What more do you want—his soul?" But I didn't. I knew it wouldn't do any good.

Months later, LaDainian and I were attending a benefit for the Boys and Girls Club in Arlington, Texas. The press interviewed him before the function began, and the *Fort Worth Star Telegram* ran the story the following day.

The article said, "Chargers Coach Norv Turner defended Tomlinson last month at the NFL owners' meetings and said the team bears some of the responsibility for putting Tomlinson on the spot. The Chargers took Tomlinson off the injury report, despite his left knee not being healed, and they failed to provide a definitive explanation for Tomlinson's absence during the game."

The article quoted LaDainian as saying, "I don't blame [the Chargers]. You've got to understand my mind-set: I have played with all kinds of injuries. So in my mind, I went through practice, and yeah, it was sore, and I knew I was going to struggle with it, but I thought I was going to play through it. . . . I felt the criticism was undeserved. At the same time, I took something good out of it. It motivated me going into the off-season and, at this point in my career, it kind of rekindled the burning inside of me to want to do even greater things."[2]

I think what hurt him most was that he could not contribute to the team. They had worked so hard to get to that place. They were fourteen and two, and in the end they could not finish.

It was almost like Moses and the Israelites getting to the Promised Land but not being able to enter. I think Dainian took the blame on his own shoulders and criticized himself for not being able to help his teammates get to the next level.

I spent the rest of that year praying for God to heal his injury so that he could continue to play—and hopefully get another chance at the play-offs and the Super Bowl.

CHAPTER 22

Moving On

LADAINIAN SPENT THE REST of the off-season focusing on healing—his heart and his knee. He did intense therapy on his knee in order to be ready for the next football season. The Chargers might have lost their Super Bowl opportunity, but he was bound and determined to work hard, get back to the play-offs, and hopefully make it to the Super Bowl.

But as the knee healed, other injuries began to show up—namely, a toe injury at the beginning of the season, then a pulled groin that stayed with him through the play-offs.

As his mother, I worry most about his injuries. If he's hurting, my first priority is to pray and get him back to playing condition. The trouble is that with my son, I don't always know when he's truly hurting. He covers it up and plays it down as much as he can. So I constantly pray, "God, You know how bad it is. Take care of him. Give him Your strength."

The next season was a difficult one for him. He got his first three-touchdown game of the season at a play-off game, and he had only 1,110 yards rushing.

I told him, "The Lord said to enjoy the journey, to be grateful for the journey."

It was a good reminder for all of us, especially when people began to talk negatively about his career. It broke my heart and often made me angry, but he didn't pay any attention. If he heard any of it, he would simply work that much harder and use it as motivation.

I know that football is a passionate game, and I know that people have strong opinions, which they are entitled to. I don't expect my story to bring about a kinder, gentler sport. But I am human, and I admit that I have been hurt by the comments of a select few. LaDainian would tell me that it's just part of the game.

As much as I would love to see Dainian make it to the Super Bowl and win, and as much as I know Dainian would love that as well, we don't pray for that. Being believers, we don't think God has a preference about who wins a football game. When someone prays, God gives that person the *strength* to play. He gives the strength to perform the skills that are already inside. He gives him victory over injuries. But I don't believe He makes one side win over another.

I don't believe God is that interested, ultimately, in who wins a football game. He's more interested in how you play the game, how you treat others, how you build your character, and how you live your life, both on and off the field. And Dainian has always understood that.

Sometimes he might get frustrated and speak his mind— like he did at the Chargers divisional play-off against the New England Patriots in January 2007. After the game, he became upset at the Patriots for performing a victory dance that mocked fellow Charger Shawne Merriman on the center-field logo at the Chargers' stadium.

And sometimes he keeps his words and thoughts to himself, as he did when he was in junior high and played one of the best games of his life up to that point. When he was pushed out of bounds on the opponent's side, some of the adults on the side-lines and in the stands called him horrible names, such as nigger and monkey. (It's harsh, isn't it, to see those hateful racial slurs in print? That's the reason I chose to repeat exactly what was said to my son, instead of using euphemisms like "the n word." I don't want the struggles he and my other kids faced to be softened. If they were strong enough to overcome these insults, we should be strong enough to remember what it was like to hear them.) When I finally found out about it, I was shocked and asked him why he never said anything about it. He simply responded, "They've been doing that ever since I first started playing football—even in Pop Warner. And it's not just me. They talk to all of us like that. People are going to say what they want to say. But it's okay, Mama. I'm used to it. It just makes me want to work harder."

He's not perfect. He has acknowledged that sometimes he pouts and has mood swings when the Chargers lose. He loves to win—but he *hates* to lose. In one moment with a reporter, he acknowledged his fear that he was becoming known as a poor sport. That concerned him because people watch him and his actions as a Christian. He told the reporter, "I don't want to get to the point where people say, 'I've seen him on the football field push a guy or say something to a guy.' The key for me is learning from the mess-ups and trying to get back on the right track."[3]

Some people have asked me why he sticks with the Chargers, why he doesn't simply ask to be traded to a team that seems to have more of a chance to make it to the Super Bowl. But he's a faithful man in his relationships and with his football teams. He stayed with TCU because he believed in that team. And he has stayed with the Chargers for the same reason. You "dance with the one who brung you," and he has never wavered in his loyalty to his teams when they were in trouble.

He has said for a long time that he wants to be a Charger for life. And loyalty is very important to him. He is still willing to take one for the team. Despite the losses, he refuses to sell out on his teammates, his coaches, the staff, his fans, or himself. Instead of talking about leaving and playing for a winner, he talks about being part of a group that turns things around. All teams have their ups and downs. And I believe all teams are winners—they may not make it to the Super Bowl, but these men are professional and very good.

"We may be banged up," he told me. "But I play with a bunch of good guys. I play for a winning team. And we refuse to give up, sell out, or shirk our responsibility to our families or our fans. You don't quit your job because things look a little bleak at times. If we go in each week, work hard, and do our part, then the team will come together and we will win. We have a strong determination. If we're playing at home, we're certainly not going to allow somebody to come into our home and beat us. And when we travel, we travel too far to lose. We go in to win."

LaDainian is grateful to the Chargers for what they've done for him, and he has never thought about looking elsewhere for the chance to get that ring before he retires.

I know that the "always the bridesmaid" feeling for him has to be difficult. Any player who loves the game as much as he does would naturally want to experience the ultimate thrill of playing in and winning the Super Bowl. But since they still haven't made it to that point, LaDainian focuses on remaining in the best shape he can and staying on top of the game so that he'll be prepared for when they *do* make it.

|||

The average running back has a career span of three years. As of this writing, Dainian is finishing his eighth season. He has begun to talk more and more about what happens after football. But it's difficult to think about, since football has always been such a deep part of his—of our whole family's—life.

We have had really good times. His career has been

awesome—greater than I think anyone ever imagined. And it has opened doors for God to use Dainian in amazing ways. When LaDainian leaves the professional football field, I know he will continue to do something connected with football, because for him, it has always been faith, family, and football.

I know he'll continue with his foundation and helping kids in the community. He may move into a position as a commentator, or he may start his own training business for players to stay in shape and work toward the combines and the draft. But I know whatever he chooses, he will do it well. That's just who he is. Dainian lives by the biblical principle of to whom much is given, much is required. He has always tried to live his life in such a way that at the end of his football career and at the end of his life, he will hear God tell him, "Well done, good and faithful servant!"

CHAPTER 23

Raising a Champion

I'VE OFTEN BEEN ASKED how I raised a champion. Was there a special diet I fed him? Was there a personal trainer and expensive equipment? Did we put him on a strict schedule?

The answer is no. Life was difficult, and sometimes tempers flared. There were times we lived on faith and little more. Some days I felt like we were living in a pressure cooker and I fought not to lose control.

I can't explain how athletic greatness thrived in that environment, but I've heard that if you put enough pressure on a piece of coal it becomes a diamond. Of course I'm not suggesting that pressure is good for a child or that my son was a lump of coal! The one thing we did have a lot of in our home was love.

The truth is that I didn't know I was raising a champion. All I knew was that he was my child, my LaDainian. And I loved him for that reason alone—not because of any skills or talents he showed.

So whenever someone asks me to give advice on the subject of raising a champion, I don't have to think too long. I say, "Look for the dream that is within your child. God has already planted the seed in him or her, and it is up to you to find that dream and nurture it."

If your child has musical talent and wants to pursue that—like my son LaVar does—don't force a football in his hands. Or if your daughter wants to play basketball or run track, don't push ballet shoes on her. It's important that the dream is *theirs*, not just yours. I have seen so many families that are unhappy because parents are trying to live their dreams through their children.

Tee and I began to listen to and observe the skills within our children when they were very young. We knew, for instance, that LaDainian wanted a weight set when he was six. We made sure he got that set and, with our supervision, used it in a healthy way.

I realize today's families are pulled in a thousand directions and everyone is busy. But the best thing you can do is watch for a talent, and if your child wants to pursue it, do whatever you can to make it happen.

In my case, money was so tight I didn't know how we were going to pay for all we needed. And often we were working so much that getting our kids where they needed to be seemed impossible. But I will never forget the look on LaDainian's face when he asked me if he could play youth football.

Herman and I attended games and practices and basically devoted our lives to our children. But that's what it takes to raise a champion, and I don't regret one minute of it.

As a parent you can do your best to raise a champion. But only your child can become that champion. You can't do it for him. Becoming a champion requires doing the right thing when no one is looking.

I've seen too many families just cast one another away, like throwing out dirty water. They don't work with one another. They act as if they can go to the meat market and pick out their mother and father and cousins and aunts and brothers. But God says to work with what He has given us, to support one another. If we can't even succeed at that, how can we succeed at the other things God calls us to do?

Watch the people your children hang out with. Those peers can make or break your children. LaDainian always chose good friends. During an interview after several years in the NFL, a reporter asked Dainian if it was easy to make friends in San Diego since he was a famous football player with a lot of money. His response was something he had always known—even before he was famous. He said, "The trick is in making the right kind of friends."[4]

When Dainian was growing up, I prayed continually for my children: that they would be safe, that they would make wise decisions, that they would grow up to be good citizens, and that they would have a strong faith in Jesus. I prayed that they would keep positive attitudes and that they would choose solid friends.

I knew God was working in the background and answering those prayers early in Dainian's life. When Dainian was in junior high, he hung around a boy who lived down the street from us. All of a sudden I didn't see the kid around anymore. I asked Dainian about it.

"He started getting in trouble," he told me. "So I can't hang around him."

"You know that you made a wise choice," I replied. "You can't afford for other kids to drag you down. You have a purpose in your life, a place to go, and you cannot let silly mistakes keep you from getting there."

It's important to impress upon children that they need to stay close to people who have their best interests at heart. They need to keep their eyes on the big picture and not let the small set-backs destroy them.

When LaDainian was up for the Heisman Trophy, he and Drew Brees both lost. But both of these men have had outstanding careers in the NFL. So I always tell children, if you don't get MVP in a game or you don't get the starting position—even when you think you deserve it—don't let it destroy you. A bad attitude can kill a dream faster than anything else.

And when the dream, passion, and talent are all in place, hold on, because God will help you with the rest. Be prepared to make sacrifices and put your ego aside for the sake of the team.

|||

LaDainian called me the other day.

"Hey, Mom," he said, "I just wanted you to know how much I appreciate all you've done for me."

I listened quietly.

"The lessons you taught me when I was growing up are the same lessons that guide me now."

I started to cry. His words meant more to me than a million dollars.

I know that when he was growing up it must have seemed like my expectations and lists of rules were endless. He tried to oblige me as much as possible because he loved me and wanted to please me, but also because he had a dream and he knew that ultimately I wanted to help him reach that dream.

While LaDainian was still in my womb, God knew the plans He had for him. And God promised to see him through to the very end. God has protected him all his life, even when I left him in Waco during his senior year of high school.

My responsibility as his parent was to see where God was working and to move my child into the place where God could continue to shape and mold him into someone who would move mountains and make a difference in this world. Really, that's what God wants for all our children—whether they have a career in football or in accounting. God has a plan for our lives, and He will work with us to see it through. That doesn't mean it will come easily! We have to work with God. We have to stay focused and strong. We have to make sacrifices. But God promises to be there with us, to help us.

For Dainian, football is where God has strategically placed him, but it wasn't easy! He had to struggle to get where he is today. Nothing was handed to him, and sometimes he had to work twice as hard as others.

There were a thousand reasons LaDainian shouldn't have made it to the NFL. There were so many obstacles in his way. People constantly told him he wasn't big enough. He came from a small town where he didn't receive the kind of training larger cities offered. The coaches were always putting him as a fullback when in his heart he knew he was a running back. But God gave him the desire and the talent. And Dainian never changed what he believed in. From the time he was nine years old, he believed and spoke the words, "I am going to college. I am going to play professional football. I will be in the NFL."

Once you set your heart on something, don't move your heart off that course. Anything that's worth having is worth the struggle. Living your dream is worth all the sweat and tears. Because, as Dainian likes to say, "If it's worth having, it's worth working for."

And as his mother, I never stopped believing in him. His dreams have always been real to me because they were always real to him. As he went from youth league to junior high and on, I often asked him, "After you finish school, then what?"

"Then I have to go to college and play football for four years."

"Then what?" I'd ask.

"Then I'm going to play for the NFL."

I don't want to make it seem like my son is perfect—he's far from it, but he *is* different. Everybody says so. And all you have to do is watch him or read about him to know that's true. I believe it's because he listened to the desires that God placed in him. And I believe it's the result of working hard, understanding the importance of professionalism and respect, and loving God.

He had a confidence to know where he wanted to take his career. But he has a humility that shines through that confidence.

Maybe it's because he understands what it's like to be the underdog. But it's also because he only has to look at his past, at what he has come through, to be reminded that ultimately it doesn't matter where you come from. If God has His hand on you, everything will work out for the good. Obstacles are nothing to God. LaDainian is living proof.

|||

So that's my story. You may wonder what's next for LT and me. Well, I'm sure he will attack his goal of winning the Super Bowl with a renewed passion. And he will continue to help and support his community wherever he sees a need. And I have my own ministries and work that I'm involved in as well.

When I thought about telling our story, I wanted to reach out to inspire and help others. But I never expected that the trip down memory lane would be so difficult. Yes, there were times when I laughed as I thought about the past. There were also times, though, that I cried. But as I revisited each hurt and painful memory, I released it, and now I feel more at peace.

My daughter-in-law and I are still LaDainian's biggest fans. And I join forces with her, as the two women who love LaDainian the most, to help him meet his goals however we can. Besides football, my life is filled with my work, church, my grandbabies, my walks with my friend Patti, and just the joy of living. But there is something else I want: I want to go home. While my journey has been amazing and I am full of memories of the people I've met and the places I've seen, my heart is calling me back to Marlin.

When Dorothy was ready to leave Oz, she only had to click the heels of her ruby slippers and repeat, "There's no place like home." Then she was transported to the life she'd known before, and nothing had changed. Her family and friends were there to embrace her, and life went on.

That is where our stories differ. I know that Marlin has changed, and my kids are grown and scattered to the four winds. Tee is buried deep in the ground in a quiet spot near Tomlinson Hill. But I suspect that if I sat still enough I could see him walking through the meadow with a fishing pole slung over his shoulder.

There's no doubt that returning would be bittersweet. The house where I grew up has long since burned down. Mom and Dad are gone, as well as my sister and best friend Bertha. She should be there, waiting to welcome me home. But she understood why I left—to give my family a better life with more opportunities.

Even though so many things have changed, that town still has a simplicity and innocence that makes me want to be there. When I go outside there, I can breathe the pure, crisp air; it's like being in a time and place that has stood still.

As I grow older, I long to go home to a place where the community is ready to welcome me back with open arms. Where I can leave my screen door unlocked and friends stop by unannounced and come in shouting, "It's me!"

Or they come up on the porch and say, "I'm passing by the store—do you need anything?" That's home.

I know it will have changed some. But LaDainian and I have begun working with a church down there to build a big community center, just like the Boys Club in Waco that drew in Dainian and started his life on the path to the NFL. I left Marlin, but when I return, I plan to bring something back to the community.

As for LaDainian, the letter he wrote me so many years ago set him directly on the road to greatness. I still keep that folded-up, now-yellowed paper with me all the time. Occasionally I'll pull it out of my purse and gaze at it in amazement—at what he has accomplished and what God has accomplished through him.

I wonder sometimes if LaDainian believes the last part of the letter, that he will make me the proudest mother in the world.

Perhaps he feels like his team must win the Super Bowl for me to feel that way.

What he doesn't realize is that that was the *very first* goal he met. As proud as I am of all his accomplishments and the way he has used his time and talents to help many, many people, there was one definitive moment when I became "the proudest mom in the whole world."

It was a hot day in Rosebud, Texas: June 23, 1979. A young nurse placed my newborn son in my arms. When our eyes and hearts met, we formed a precious, lifelong bond. That was the beginning of a shared love that was strong enough to endure anything. I can still feel him in my arms when I think about that moment.

As I held my baby so tenderly, I knew there were bills to pay, jobs to go to, and others who needed my attention. And destiny might have been calling even then. But at that instant, when I looked down at my tiny son, there was no one else in the world but LT and me.

LIFE AND PARENTING LESSONS

- Just telling your child something isn't good for him isn't always enough. Oftentimes you have to help your child visually associate that thing with something memorable to drive home your point.
- Pay attention to those clues that set your child apart—even at a young age, those things matter. They are hints of what God has in mind for him or her.
- All children need clear-cut, well-established boundaries. They need to know how far they can go.
- Watch your children and look for their skills and interests—not the ones you want them to have, but the ones they already possess. Then encourage them in those skills. Dainian's passion was football. His younger brother's wasn't. LaVar used to love writing poetry, and he had tablets full of poems. I wasn't that interested in poetry, but I encouraged him to continue—even though I really didn't understand what the poems meant! They made sense to him. Spend time studying your children. Get to know them and see what motivates them. Then encourage that.
- Celebrate your children regardless of the kind of job

they do. One year Dainian was having such a hard time with his front line that every yard he got was a struggle. And I would say, "Those were some hard yardages to get. But, hey, you got over a hundred. Congratulations!" Find the good to celebrate and appreciate.

- Take the time to instill strong character qualities in your children. When I see Dainian focused and controlling his temper when he plays football, I wonder if his father's stories instilled those qualities in him. There is no telling how much Tee's tales and actions molded my sons into the men they are today.
- Keep perspective on the things that are important; let the other things go.
- The best thing you can do for your children is to pray for them. Ultimately, you have no control over your child. But God watches over those we pray for. And He can shape and mold a heart and attitude much better than we can!

THE MARLIN COMMUNITY CENTER

LADAINIAN, TORSHA, AND I are working with Bible Way Church Family Worship Center in Marlin to build a place where people can stay connected with others.

We want to offer something for everybody, from children to seniors. The center will include a library with tutoring, a bowling alley, and basketball and tennis courts. Everything that keeps a child off the streets and out of trouble.

Part of the proceeds from this book will go toward making the community center in Marlin a reality. To make a donation, contact S. Strother at Trustworthy Consulting, 254-644-7057 or trustworthy.consulting@yahoo.com.

THE TOMLINSON TOUCHING LIVES FOUNDATION

LADAINIAN HAS ALWAYS BELIEVED in the importance of education. Before he started the Tomlinson Touching Lives Foundation, he wanted to make sure he was a strong role model for kids. He knew part of that was to complete his own college education, since he had pulled out his last semester to train for the combines. So during the off-season he finished his schooling and received his college degree.

Now he awards scholarships. Proceeds from LaDainian's annual golf tournament help support his "School is Cool" program, which awards thirty college scholarships each year. Fifteen scholarships go to kids from San Diego, and fifteen go to students from his alma mater, University High School in Waco. He also sends seven students from Morse High School to a seminar at Columbia University, where they get entrepreneurial training.

LaDainian and Torsha feel God has placed a strong responsibility on them to help others. The foundation gives Dainian the opportunity to really connect with those he helps. At each Chargers home game, for instance, he hosts the 21 Club, where he invites twenty-one kids from San Diego youth groups and nonprofit organizations to attend a game. Afterward, he invites the children down to the field, where they get photos and a one-on-one visit with their football hero. He always sends the kids home with goody bags that contain school supplies and other treats.

Talking with the kids after the games has always been really important to Dainian. When I see him smiling and posing with each child for a picture, I know he is doing it because he genuinely loves those kids and wants to make a difference in their lives. Even when he is worn out and in pain—after every game he goes home and sits in a tub of ice to fight the abuse his body has taken—he believes the interaction with the kids is more important than his discomfort.

The fishing trip that he sponsors every year is for the Monarch School for homeless and at-risk teens in San Diego. I often wonder if he started that part of the foundation because he remembered the day I gathered all the kids and took them on their first fishing trip or if it was because of that Christian youth camp he attended where he met all those displaced kids. Maybe it's both.

The Thanksgiving meals are something he and Torsha look forward to as well. Perhaps he thinks about his TCU days—when he would bring home fellow football players who couldn't get to their families—as he passes out more than two thousand complete Thanksgiving dinners to the disadvantaged in San Diego.

"Mom, I'd never seen so many people!" he told me in 2008. "And they were all truly in need." Dainian and Torsha just hugged them and cried with them. "So many of them didn't know what they were going to do or how they were going to make it."

And when he gives disadvantaged children hundreds of pairs of shoes, maybe his mind goes back to the days when new shoes were a special gift. I remember when Dainian and LaVar were little and still at the Boys Club in Waco. Nike had given all the kids shoes and passed them out there. That affected LaDainian deeply, because he had been the recipient, and was now able to be the one to give. And he remembers how a good pair of shoes would last longer and instill a little confidence and hope in a child.

But of all of the charity work LaDainian and Torsha do, the Christmas program brings them an extra measure of joy. Every Christmas Dainian personally gives away more than 1,500 presents to young patients at San Diego's children's hospital and health center.

Although CBS's *60 Minutes* captured the work he does there, he doesn't do it to receive publicity. Most of the time he sneaks in with no cameras or publicity and spends time with the children.

But *60 Minutes* did catch a moving scene when a beaming LT knelt down beside a little girl in a wheelchair and offered her a big white teddy bear.

As he handed her the stuffed animal, he said, "This is for you, my princess."

ABOUT THE AUTHORS

Loreane Tomlinson was born into a rural life on the outskirts of Marlin, Texas. The small house she shared there with her parents, three sisters, and a brother lacked many modern conveniences. But the children were raised on the Bible, strong discipline, and a lot of love. These principles forged a strong drive in her that she carried into her adult life.

However, the simple country life Loreane knew and loved did not prepare her for the changes she would face while raising her own three children, Londria, LaDainian, and LaVar. Especially when LaDainian's love of football catapulted him into the position of superstar running back of the San Diego Chargers, taking her with him every step of the way. Never in her wildest dreams did she expect to be on television programs like *60 Minutes*, or to be making commercials for the likes of Campbell's soup and Vizio, or to be giving countless interviews to radio stations and publications like *Sports Illustrated*.

Loreane currently lives in Fort Worth, Texas, is an ordained minister, and dabbles in real estate. One of her happiest roles is that of "Granny" to her five grandchildren. Still LaDainian's number-one fan, she adds the title of author to her résumé as she presents her first book, *LT & Me*.

Patti M. Britton is a native Texan currently living in Fort Worth. She received a bachelor's degree from the University of Texas at Arlington, where she studied English and sociology. She is married to Carl Britton, and they have one daughter, Lori. Patti comes from a long line of published writers and is proud to join their ranks.

Her journey with Loreane Tomlinson began with a chance meeting on the wooded walking trails in Fort Worth, Texas. Three years later, Mrs. Tomlinson said to her, "God told me to ask you to cowrite my book, *LT & Me*. If you don't write it, it won't be written." So their collaboration began on the same trail as their friendship. Through the heat, cold, wind, and rain, they laughed and cried together as Loreane's story unfolded. It is with great pride that she submits her contribution to the saga, *LT & Me*.

Ginger Kolbaba is an editor of discipleship and women's resources, including *Today's Christian Woman* magazine and MarriagePartnership.com. She has been a columnist for *Let's Worship* and has published more than 250 articles. Also an accomplished book author, Ginger has written or contributed to fifteen books, including her most recent novel series, Secrets from Lulu's Café, which includes *Desperate Pastors' Wives*, *A Matter of Wife and Death*, and *Katt's in the Cradle*.

Ginger also teaches and speaks across the country. She has appeared on national venues such as CNN's *Nancy Grace* and Court TV's *Catherine Crier Live*, as well as Family Life Radio and Moody Radio's *Midday Connection*. When she isn't chained to her computer, Ginger enjoys spending time with her husband motorcycling through the countryside, visiting Yellowstone National Park, walking her Doberman, reading good books, and talking theory with her friends about the television series *Lost*.

NOTES

1   Kevin Acee, "Tomlinson Puts Football in Perspective," *San Diego Union-Tribune*, August 4, 2005.
2. Charean Williams, "A Motivated LT Ready to Run," *Fort Worth Star-Telegram*, May 1, 2008.
3. Kevin Acee, "Better than Ever?" *Pro Football Guide 2008* (Indian Trail, NC: Sports Spectrum Publishing, 2008).
4. LaDainian Tomlinson, interview by Carlos Watson, *Conversations with Carlos Watson*, Hearst-Argyle Television, Inc., November 2007.